Butterfield Overland National Historic Trail
Through
Arkansas' Pope & Conway Counties

1858-1861
Featuring Over 100 Color Photographs and Maps

by
Bob Crossman

Background image is the Butterfield Historic Trail in Menifee between Cadron Ferry and Plummer's Station in Conway County

Butterfield Overland National Historic Trail Through Arkansas' Pope & Conway Counties

This is the only daguerreotype or photographic image of a Celerity wagon actually used by the Butterfield Overland Mail Co. This image was taken near the Cottonwood Stage Station, El Paso, Texas in early 1861. The driver in the 'ten gallon hat' was David McLaughlin. Image courtesy of the Nita Stewart Haley Memorial Library at Midland, Texas. The image above has been flipped horizontally, which now accurately shows the driver and brake on the right hand side of the Celerity wagon.

Explore the BUTTERFIELD OVERLAND NATIONAL HISTORIC TRAIL by reading these books by Bob Crossman:

 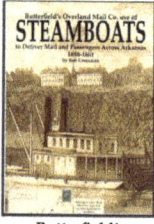   

| Butterfield's Overland Mail Co. STAGECOACH TRAIL Across Arkansas | Butterfield's Overland Mail Co. use of STEAMBOATS to Deliver Mail and Passengers Arkansas | POSTAL HISTORY of John Butterfield's Overland Mail Co. on the Southern & Central Routes including Butterfield's Pony Express | Butterfield's Overland Mail Co. as REPORTED in Arkansas Newspapers of 1858-1861 | Butterfield's Overland National Historic Trail PASSENGER DIARIES & STORIES Across Oklahoma, Arkansas and Missouri |

© 2024 Robert O. Crossman
Ingram Spark Press
ISBN 979-8-9885900-6-4 Hard Cover
ISBN 979-8-9885900-7-1 Paper Cover
July 19, 2024

Butterfield Overland National Historic Trail Through Arkansas' Pope & Conway Counties

Table of Contents

Introduction 4

CHAPTER ONE
A Few Details To Understand the Larger Story 7
   A Brief History of the Overland Mail Company 8
   John Butterfield, President of the Overland Mail Co. ... 10
   How Butterfield Established this Historic Trail 12
   Construction of the Trail Through These Counties 14
   Types of Stages Used by the Overland Mail Co. 23
   Butterfield's Steamboat, *Jennie Whipple* 26
   Sub-contractor J. T. Chidester, Reeside & Co. 33
   Brief Description of the Memphis to Ft. Smith Route . 38

CHAPTER TWO
Discovering The Trail Through Conway County .. 53
   Plummer Station 65
   Lewisburg Station 89

Discovering The Trail Through Pope County 147
   Hurricane Station 156
   Potts Inn Station 167
   Norristown Station & the Dardanelle Ferry 206

CHAPTER THREE
Brief Description of the Entire 3,000 Mile Route 223

About the Author 231

For Additional Reading 233

ಐಖ

© 2024 Robert O. Crossman

INTRODUCTION

In the following pages, you will find a report of the author's four year search through Conway and Pope counties as he explored the disappearing route once taken by the Butterfield Overland Mail Company stagecoaches as they sped from Memphis to San Francisco.

Why, you may ask, is this search worthy of such an effort? From September of 1858 to March of 1861, Arkansas was a vital link in the longest stagecoach line in the world. The importance of this route is reflected in the January 2023 decision of the U. S. Congress and President Biden to declare this route "THE BUTTERFIELD OVERLAND NATIONAL HISTORIC TRAIL."

This NATIONAL HISTORIC TRAIL played a vital role as it

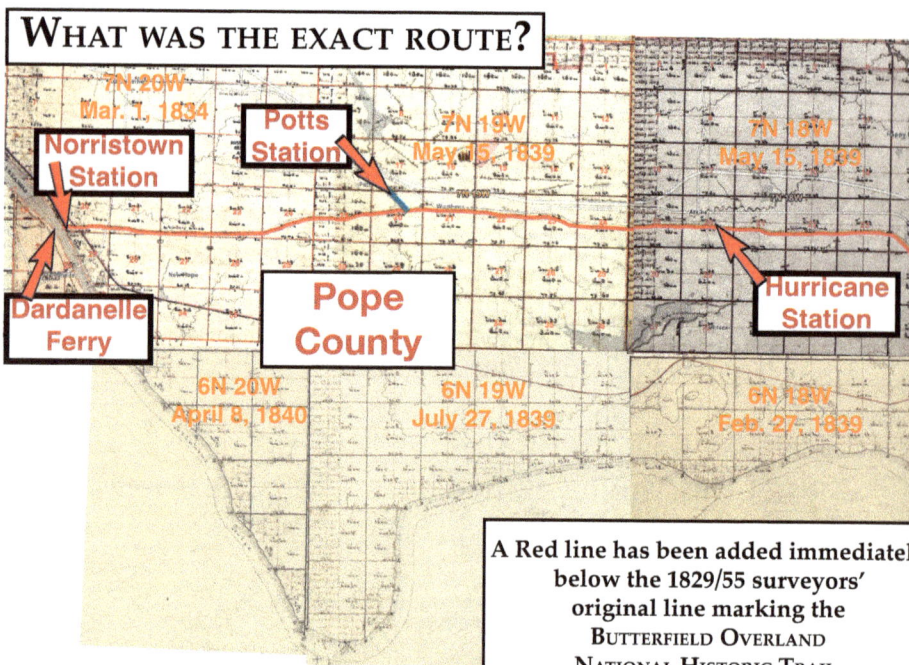

A Red line has been added immediately below the 1829/55 surveyors' original line marking the BUTTERFIELD OVERLAND NATIONAL HISTORIC TRAIL.

Source: Bureau of Land Management(BLM), General Land Office (GLO) Maps based on surveys 1829 to 1855

© 2024 Robert O. Crossman

drastically improved communication and transportation between California and the east coast.

Susan Dragoo, in her new book, *"Finding the Butterfield,"* eloquently describes the situation: *"In the second decade of the twenty-first century, with the instantaneous nature of communications, it is difficult to grasp just how significant it was in the 1850's when, before either a telegraph line or a railroad spanned the North American continent, a stagecoach operation created the first rapid communication and transportation link across the United States, moving mail and passengers over land at record speed and paving the way toward the ultimate goal of a transcontinental railroad.*

New York Herald reporter Waterman Lilly Ormsby, Jr., the only through passenger on the first westbound Butterfield stage, wrote:

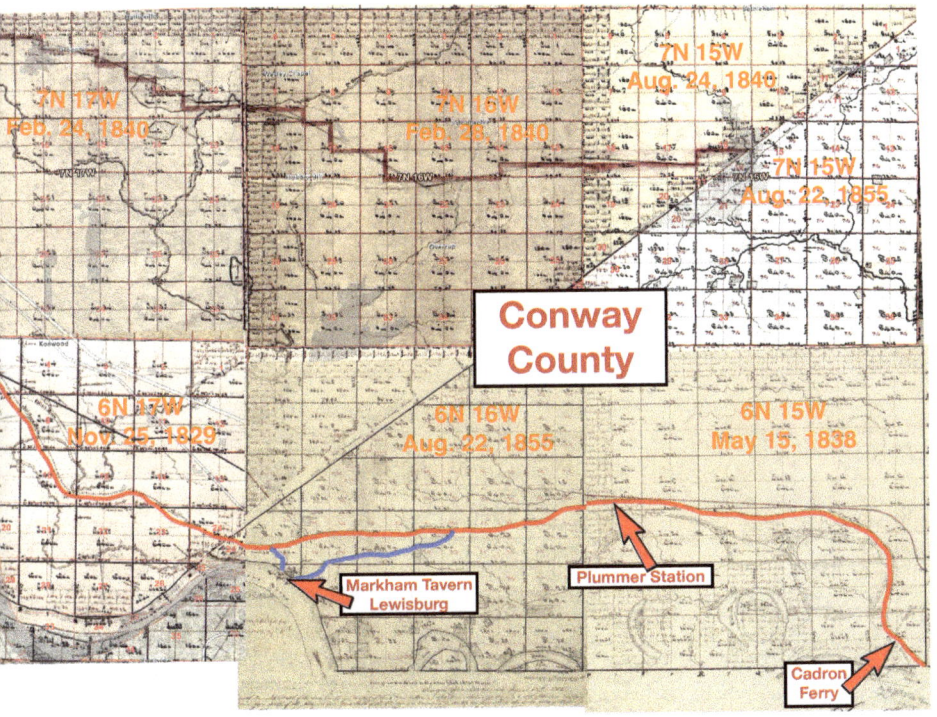

© 2024 Robert O. Crossman

> 'I looked forward in my imagination to the time when, instead of a wagon road to the Pacific, we should have a railroad, and when, instead of having to wait over forty days for an answer from San Francisco, a delay of as many minutes will be looked upon as a gross imposition, and of as many seconds as 'doing from fair to middling.'
>
> His prescient contemplation anticipated not only the coming of the railroad but also our modern expectations for the speed of communication." (Finding the Butterfield: A Journey through Time in Indian Territory, by Susan Dragoo, 2024, pages 7-8)

In the following pages you will find the first chapter describing a few details that will help the reader understand the larger story of this historic trail.

The second chapter will report the author's four year search through Conway and Pope counties for the disappearing route now called THE BUTTERFIELD NATIONAL HISTORIC TRAIL.

The final chapter will briefly describe the entire 3,000 mile trail from the Mississippi River to the west coast of California.

The reader is invited to explore the author's additional books on THE BUTTERFIELD OVERLAND NATIONAL HISTORIC TRAIL:
- Butterfield's Overland Mail Co. STAGECOACH Trail Across Arkansas
- Butterfield's Overland Mail Co. use of STEAMBOATS to Deliver Mail and Passengers Across Arkansas
- Butterfield's Overland Mail Co. as REPORTED in Arkansas Newspapers of 1858-1861
- POSTAL HISTORY of John Butterfield's Overland Mail Co. on the Southern & Central Routes including Butterfield's Pony Express
- Butterfield Overland National Historic Trail PASSENGER DIARIES & STORIES across Oklahoma, Arkansas & Missouri
- Butterfield Overland National Historic Trail Through FAULKNER COUNTY, Arkansas.

Butterfield Overland National Historic Trail Through Arkansas' Pope & Conway Counties

A Few Details To Understand The Larger Story...

The Butterfield stagecoaches delivered mail cross country twice a week in less than 25 days. Previously, mail to California by steamship was twice a month and could take 30 to 50+ days.

The Old Routes:

Map 9 – Via Tehuantepec Contract Route and Via Panama Contract Route
Via Nicaragua Private Mail Route

Map courtesy of Richard Frajola, "The Routes" page 5

Prior to the Butterfield contract, mail delivery to California involved slow and tedious bi-monthly steamship routes involving crossing land at Panama, Nicaragua or Tehuantepec.

Image courtesy of Silver Dollar City

OVERLAND MAIL CO.
1858-1864

The gold rush of 1848 began a mass migration of men to California, seeking fortune for themselves and their families back home. This migration put increasing pressure on Congress to improve mail delivery to and from the Pacific coast.

Bidding against eight others, John Butterfield was chosen September 16, 1857, by former Tennessee Governor, the Postmaster General Aaron Brown for a new Route #12578. The six year contract, with a $600,000 annual payment, required Butterfield to carry mail and passengers, semi-weekly departing simultaneously from St. Louis & Memphis, merging in Fort Smith, then on to San Francisco, in 25 days or less in comfortable four-horse stagecoaches.

In only 12 months, the Overland Mail Co. poured about $3,500,000.00 into establishing the 3,000 mile route from the Mississippi River to the Pacific coast. Butterfield purchased 34 mail stagecoaches and 66 Celerity wagons from J. S. and E. A. Abbot of Concord New Hampshire, 1,800 horses (avg. of $98/head) and mules (avg. of $102/head), and ordered delivery of 3,000 tons of grain and hay to the various stations along the route.

In the beginning of service, Butterfield established 139 stations about 15 miles apart, increasing to 175 stations within a year - at prices varying from $125 to $175 per quarter. The 34 mail stagecoaches, Celerity wagons, and 150 other vehicles, were spread along the 3,134 mile route, (including a year later, in August 1859, the 322 miles from Memphis to Fort Smith).

John Butterfield employed almost 2,000 drivers, conductors, station-keepers, blacksmiths, mechanics, wheelwrights, helpers, hostlers, herders, veterinarians, armed guards, and harness makers along the route.

True to the contract, in mid-September, 1858, almost simultaneously the Overland Mail departed San Francisco, St. Louis and Memphis — arriving at their destinations in less than 25 days.

On March 20, 1860, the Overland Mail Company Board decided to retain its structure, but remove John Butterfield as president. William B. Dinsmore was elected president in Butterfield's place.

After 130 weeks of operation on the southern route and with the dawn of the Civil War in March of 1861, the Southern Route was canceled. Legally unable to cancel Butterfield's old six year contract, the Postmaster General 'moved' the contract's location north to the Central Route, entirely avoiding the southern states. This required John Butterfield to begin moving employees and equipment north to the Placerville — Salt Lake City — St. Joseph route.

Starting July 1, 1861, the new Central Route contract required daily trips from St. Joseph, Missouri to Placerville, California. It also required Butterfield to oversee the once private Pony Express over that same route.

In mid 1864 when the six year contract was complete, John Butterfield ended his relationship with the Overland Mail Co. In August 1864, former board president Wm. Dinsmore, organized a new Overland Mail Co. and continued seeking postal contracts. In December 1866, the Overland Mail Co. and several other stage lines were purchased by Ben Holladay. Within a few months, Holladay sold his entire stagecoach business to Wells Fargo & Company.

JOHN BUTTERFIELD
November 18, 1801 – November 14, 1869

Bidding against eight others, John Butterfield was chosen September 16, 1857, by former Tennessee Governor, the Postmaster General Aaron Brown, for a new Route #12578 – that would become the future BUTTERFIELD OVERLAND NATIONAL HISTORIC TRAIL.

Concerning the selection of John Butterfield's bid over the competition, Gerald T. Ahnert, historian and authority on the Overland Mail Company, wrote: "What was needed was someone with some of the most extensive experience in the United States." [Source: "Butterfield Makes the Southern Overland Trail His Own, Gerald T. Ahnert, Overland Journal, Spring, 2020, pg. 13.]

Born in Berne, New York in 1801, Butterfield grew up on a farm located directly on a stagecoach route. By the age of 19, John was driving spring coaches for the Thorpe & Sprague Livery Stable in Albany. Moving to Utica, he married Malinda Baker in 1822, eventually having eight children. To make ends meet, he moonlighted at night driving a two-seat carriage. In 1825, John became manager of Parker and Co. Soon his enterprise grew into a boarding house, eastern stagecoach lines, packet boats and railroads.

"He had been a stagecoach driver when a young man, and had risen to be owner of nearly all the stage lines running in Western New York. In 1849 he was engaging in transporting freight across the Isthmus of Panama. He was also projector of the Morse Telegraph line between Buffalo and New York, and he not only built it, but also put it into successful operation. Enlisting others with him, he founded a line of Lake Ontario and St. Lawrence steamers, and in 1849 he formed the express company of Butterfield, Wasson and Co. We suppose he may claim to be founder of the American Express Company, for in 1850 he approached Henry Wells with the acceptable proposition that the three firms should be consolidated." *[Source: Harper's New Monthly Magazine, Aug., 1875, p. 322]*

In 1857, by the time John Butterfield was fifty-six he "had accumulated a comfortable fortune, and it was widely known that no man in the country knew more about the ins and outs of horse-drawn transportation. He had an incredible memory and was a natural born leader, admired because of his basic generosity and genuine interest in public benefit. He was scrupulously fair... besides being deeply religious...

A busy man in the field of stagecoach lines and transportation, Butterfield was able to attract and keep good workers. A successful businessman, he didn't seek glory and glamour but was much more interested in results. He had little formal education, but he made up for it with his natural organizational and managerial talents...

At a time when he should have retired to enjoy comfortable life with a comfortable fortune behind him, Butterfield instead chose to commit himself to the most outstanding achievement of his career: the Overland Mail Company..." *[Source: "Butterfield Makes the Southern Overland Trail His Own, Gerald T. Ahnert, Overland Journal, Spring, 2020, pg. 13.]*

ഈᏣ

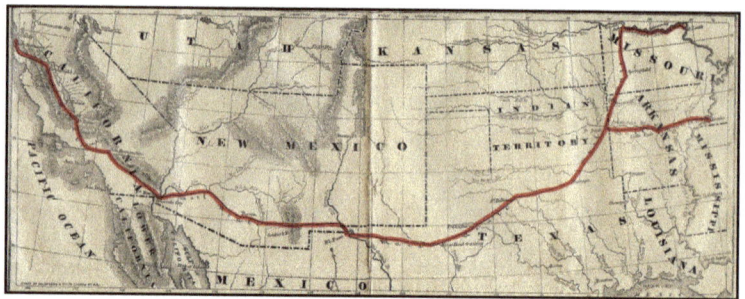

How Butterfield Established the Trail

On September 16, 1857, John Butterfield signed a contract with Postmaster General Aaron Brown for a new Postal Route #12578. That contract required the Overland Mail Co. to establish a route: *"from the Mississippi River to San Francisco, California, converging at Little Rock, Arkansas; thence, via Preston, Texas, or as near so as may be found advisable, to the best point of crossing the Rio Grande above El Paso, and not far from Fort Fillmore; thence, along the new road being opened and constructed under the direction of the Secretary of the Interior, to or near Fort Yuma, California; thence, through the best passes and along the best valleys for safe and expeditious staging, to San Francisco, California, and back, twice a week, in good four horse post coaches or spring wagons suitable for the conveyance of passengers as well as the safety and security of the mails..."*

John Butterfield received permission for the St. Louis and Memphis stages to merge at Fort Smith instead of Little Rock, Arkansas.

From the Mississippi to Fort Smith, existing roads would be used. To determine the exact route west of Fort Smith, two expeditions were sent out by the Overland Mail Company on January 2, 1858.

Marquis Kenyon, Frank DeRyther, S. L. Nellis, James Swart and John Butterfield, Jr. began their expedition out of San Francisco.

George Wood, Jesse Talcott and Charles P. Cole began their expedition out of St. Louis. The two expeditions would meet at El Paso, Texas.

Completing their expeditions, they returned to Fort Smith on April 24, 1858, *"having made the trip from El Paso – a distance of 925 miles – in the unprecedented short time of twenty-five days, which we believe is the quickest trip ever made across the Plains."* (May 1, 1858 Arkansas Gazette)

On this return trip to St. Louis, Marquis L. Kenyon made significant changes to the route recommended by the westbound expedition.

In June of 1858, with the preliminary survey complete: 1) a team began in California and another in Fort Smith, renting existing buildings or constructing new buildings to serve as stations; 2) horses, equipment and spare replacement stages and stagecoaches were distributed along the route; and 3) Daniel Butterfield fixed the schedule, setting arrival and departures to the minute from each of the major stations.

Butterfield established 139 stations in the beginning of service averaging about 15 miles apart, increasing to 175 stations within a year. The 34 mail stagecoaches, the 66 Celerity wagons, and 150 other vehicles were spread along the route. John Butterfield employed almost 2,000 drivers, conductors, station-keepers, blacksmiths, mechanics, wheelwrights, helpers, hostlers, herders, veterinarians, armed guards, and harness makers along the route.

True to the contract, in mid September, 1858, almost simultaneously, the Overland Mail departed San Francisco, St. Louis and Memphis — arriving at their destinations in less than 25 days.

As the months passed, there were several adjustments made to the route, but the overall trail remained the same until it was relocated north to the Central Route (St. Joseph, Missouri, via Salt Lake to Placerville, California) in the spring of 1861.

Segment of Military Road west of Cadron Creek
16' wide, ditches on both sides

CONSTRUCTION OF HISTORIC TRAIL

Note: Before Arkansas became a state in 1836, most roads in Arkansas were little more than animal paths. In order to transfer troops quickly between Little Rock's Fort Pike and Fort Gibson in Indian Territory, Congress approved the construction of a road between Memphis, Little Rock, Fort Smith, and Fort Gibson. Construction began about 1828, and was completed in 1836.

To pass through Conway and Pope Counties, the Butterfield Overland Mail stagecoaches traveled primarily on the 1827 Military Road instead of attempting to blaze a new trail.

The construction of the 1827 road from Little Rock to Fort Smith and on to Fort Gibson was a pet project of Henry W. Conway, delegate to Congress from the Arkansas Territory. In Washington DC on January 26, 1825, he addressed the House of Representatives: *"The frontier of this country is much exposed to the Indians and it is necessary to have a good road. The appropriation asked for is sufficient to make a wagon road. The land lies high and dry; and the advantages will be direct communication with the States east of the Mississippi and an increase of the value of the public lands. It will be a continuation of the Memphis road, which was authorized at the last session, and would form part of the communication with Santa Fe. It is, therefore, of great importance."* [Arkansas Gazette, March 8, 1825]

The house passed the bill the next day, and President John Quincy Adams signed the bill March 3, 1825.

It was expected that the work of surveying and

marking the route of the Little Rock to Fort Gibson Road would take two or three months. A portion of that study refers to route between Fort Smith and Little Rock:

[All mileage notations below refer to the number of miles from Fort Gibson in Indian Territory.] **1825**

> 60 miles, Arkansas river, at Fort Smith —The country is gently rolling and somewhat stony, to a lake in the bottom near the river, which appears to have once been the bed of the Arkansas. —This lake or pond is surrounded by first rate bottom land; timber, oak, gum, elm, ash and walnut; undergrowth, cane. —From thence to the Arkansas, the bottom is rich and never subject to inundation. The road crosses to the south side of the Arkansas, and a ferry will be required at all seasons.
>
> 74 miles, Big Vash Grass creek —with the exception of two small prairies, the country is gently rolling woodland; timber, oak, hickory, & c. This is a considerable stream, running northeast, over which a bridge will be necessary, the probable cost of which will be about $300. The route lies through some low and wet lands, where a causeway of half a mile will be required.
>
> 78 miles, Big creek —part prairie, low and rather wet; the remainder gently rolling woodland. A bridge will be necessary across this creek. Timber for that purpose is abundant, and the banks good; probable expense of erecting it, about $150.
>
> 94 miles, Six Mile creek — country mostly prairie, some woodland, gently rolling, timber post oak & c. A good crossing can be made across this creek, but a bridge would be preferable.
>
> 98 miles, Three Mile creek—gently rolling wood-land; a small stream, and crossing good.
>
> 100 miles, Short Mountain creek—country a little rolling, timber oak, & c. This is a considerable stream, and a bridge will be required, which will cost about $300.
>
> 116 miles, Rocky bayou, or Shoal Creek—part prairie, but mostly wood-land; timber, oak, black jack & c.' crossing good.

119 miles, Little Shoal creek.

134 miles, Arkansas river, at Dardanelles—country gently rolling, part hilly, and some prairie; timber, oak, pine, & c.

The Commissioners were induced to choose this route, in preference to continuing down on the south side of the Arkansas, in consequence of the difficulties which they would have encountered, or rather the impossibility of finding a suitable point to cross the Petit Jean bayou, and mountain of the same name, where a road could not be made except at a very great expense, and even then not without extending the distance. Besides these objections, they would have had to encounter other nearly equal obstructions at the Fourche LeFevre and the Big and Little Maumelle bayous, and other small streams, most of which would require expensive bridges; and the face of the country being very broken and stony, made it impossible to find a route where a good road could be constructed without immense labor and expense.

141 miles, **Gally creek**—a bridge required to across a small meiry stream on this route; country gently rolling; timber, oak, hickory & c.; good ford across the creek.

156 miles, **Point Remove creek**—country gently rolling, part level, some low grounds; a causeway of a few yards will be required in one place, across a cypress swamp; timber, oak, gum, ash, hickory & c. A bridge will be required across this creek, which will cost about $300, or a ferry may be established by bestowing considerable labor in improving the landing.

160 miles, **Cherokee boundary line.**

166 miles, **Gap Creek.**

174 miles, **Cadron Creek**—country part gently rolling, and part low and wet; some causeways will be required, but only for short distances; timber, oak, gum, etc. This is a considerable stream, which will require a bridge at an expense of about $400; it may be forded when at low stages.

191 miles, Palarm bayou—country, broken; timber, oak, hickory, pine, etc. A bridge, which will cost about $250, will be required on this bayou.

> 198 miles, White Oak bayou.
> 207 miles and 70 chains, Arkansas river, opposite Little Rock —country part hilly, and part low land; timber, oak, pine & c.
> Across the Arkansas to Little Rock is 17 chains and 72 links, making total distance from Cantonment Gibson to Little Rock 208 miles, 7 chains, and 72 links.   [Arkansas Gazette, Jan. 3, 1826, page 3]

In the July 3, 1827 issue of the *Arkansas Gazette*, an advertisement was printed seeking bids on the work.

> "The road will be opened on the route designated by the Commissioners, which is blazed and marked throughout the whole distance, and is to be cut in ranges as long and direct as a reference of the line of the Commissioners, and the general direction of the survey, will admit of. **It will be cut full sixteen feet wide.** The timber, brush, drift, rocks, and every species of obstruction, are to be cleared from the surface, and all holes to be filled up, so as to render the passage smooth and easy. **Large sized trees** must be cut off within one foot of the ground, and the stumps centers hollowed outward; and saplings, at no more than 3 inches. **In marshes**, swamps, and bogs, a causeway [corduroy road] is to be constructed, and the whole width of the road, to be made of rails or poles, 4 inches in diameter at the small end. They must be laid compactly together, perpendicular to the line of direction, and covered with a layer of about 12 inches of solid earth in the middle, and 6 inches on the sides, of the causeway. Substantial riders of durable timber, must be pinned on each side of the causeway, in such parts of the road, as is liable to be subjected to the effects of overflow. **A ditch** must be dug on the sides of the causeway, 18 inches wide and 12 inches deep. In prairie land, which is liable to be boggy in wet seasons, a ditch of a similar kind must be dug on each side of the road, and the earth removed and thrown on the road, in such a manner as to raise it in the center.
> All **hills** and small elevations, on the line of the road, are to be sloped off each way, so as to permit wagons, etc. to pass

> with convenience.
> The **banks of all creeks**, branches, streams, and ravines, on the route, are to be dug down so as to render the ascent and descent safe and easy at all seasons of the year.

The January 8, 1828 issue of the *Arkansas Gazette* reported: *"whole of the road from this place to Cantonment Gibson is completed, with the exception of 35 miles, which will be immediately put under contract, and also of a few places (of only a few rods in length) on which the contractors will be required to do a little more work...."*

THE LITTLE ROCK TO MEMPHIS ROAD

Concerning the road from Little Rock to Memphis, similar orders were issued January 27th 1826 to Lt. F. L. Griffith:

"SIR, You have been selected to superintend the making of a road from a point on the West Bank of the river Mississippi, opposite the town of Memphis in the state of Tennessee, to Little Rock in the Territory of Arkansas, authorized by an act of Congress approved the 31st of January 1824..

*The road is to be opened in reaches staked out as straight as practicable, keeping a view the general direction of the survey, in the ascent and declivities of hills, and other localities, which cause a necessary deviation from a straight line. It is to be at least **twenty four feet wide** throughout, and all timber, brushwood, and other rubbish or impediments, are to be removed from it, and all holes within its limits are to be filled with earth. The **stumps** must be cut as low to the ground as practicable, their height in no instance to exceed two thirds of their diameter, they should be hollowed towards the center in cutting them to retain the rain and moisture...*
[*"Documentary History of Arkansas, 2nd Edition, Univ of Arkansas Press, 2013]*

The Fort Smith to Little Rock portion was basically complete by the spring of 1828.

The Memphis to Little Rock portion was not completed until 1836.

Prior to the Butterfield Overland National Historic Trail

The 1827 Memphis to Fort Smith Military Roads discussed above were not the first roads built in Arkansas.

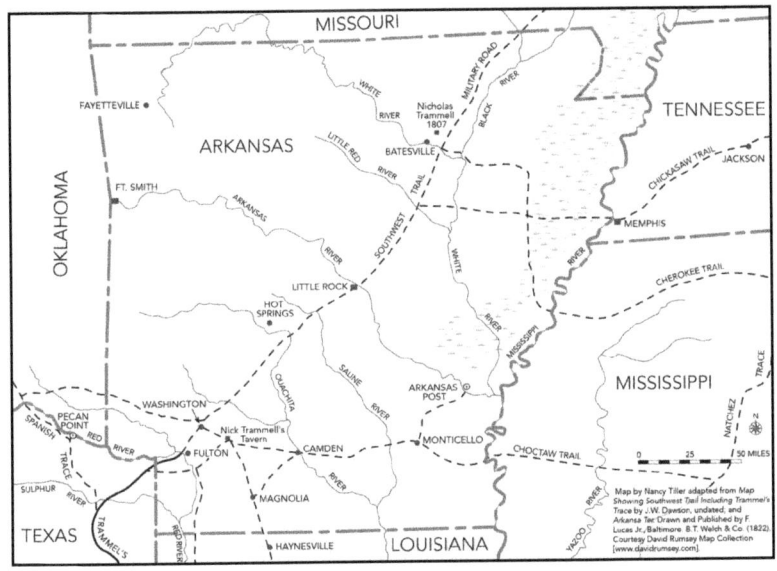

Southwest Trail
Map by Nancy Tiller adapted from map showing the Southwest Trail by J. W. Dawson and the 1822"Arkansa" map by F. Lucas, Jr.

One of the first routes in Arkansas was the **Southwest Trail**. It was an old Indian Trail that began at St. Genevieve, 60 miles south of St. Louis, entering the northeast corner of Arkansas Territory north of Pocahontas. From there it angled across the state, via Little Rock, toward the southwest corner. In 1803 Congress appropriated funds to improve that route. After 1831, when Congress appropriated $15,000 for improvements, the road was often called the "National Road" or "Military Road."

The map above also shows the **Chickasaw Trail** entering Arkansas at Memphis. Also, entering through Mississippi, it shows the **Cherokee Trail** leading to

Batesville. Across southern Arkansas this map shows the route of the **Choctaw Trail** through Monticello.

John C. Benedict, an early Faulkner County resident, traveled on the Southwest trail in 1818, immigrating from Missouri to Cadron. In places they had to cut and clear trees to allow their small wagon to pass. Near Heber Springs they left the wagon behind and followed an obscure trail to Cadron. *[Arkansas Frontier, p.114]*

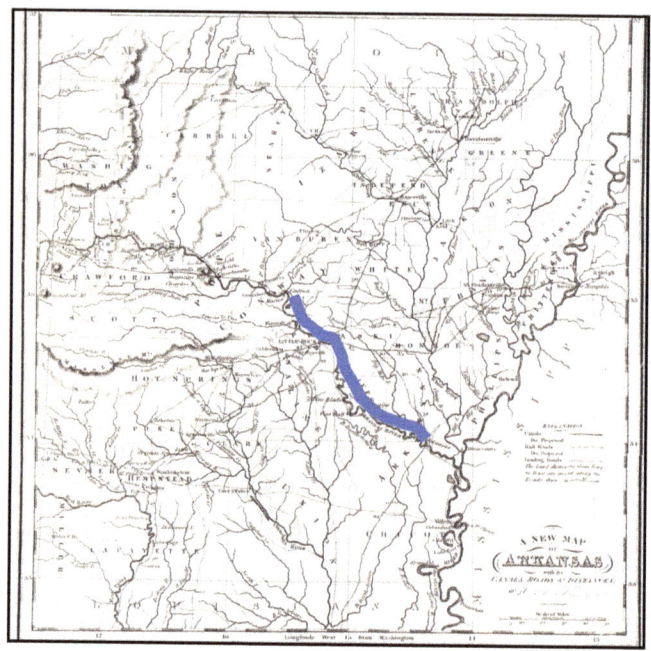

Cadron-Arkansas Post Road also known as Pyeatt's Road
1836 Arkansas, by Henry Schenck Tanner, blue added over road shown

The first road constructed by Arkansas labor was known as John **Pyeatt's Road** *(also referred to as the "Cadron to Arkansas Post Road.")* About 1807 Pyeatt enlisted his neighbors to construct a road from Cadron (in Faulkner County) following the north bank of the Arkansas River to connect with an old Indian Trail at Grand Prairie that led directly to Arkansas Post.

These roads, along with the 1827 Memphis to Fort Smith Road, were not smooth and paved. Rather, the brush and trees had been cleared, leaving low stumps behind. Only light wagons and horses could travel on these routes, and they "often became totally impassable during rainy seasons." *[Historical Review - Volume Two, April 2004, Arkansas State Highway Department. page 5-7]*

One traveler on the Southwest Trail near Fulton in 1834 described the road as being filled with rocks, stumps and fallen trees that travelers would detour around, eventually wandering back to the original route. *[Historical Review - Volume Two, April 2004, Arkansas State Highway Department. page 7]*

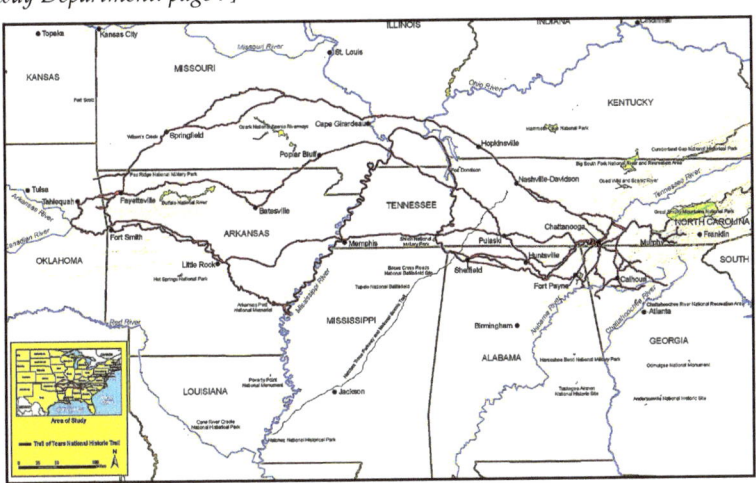

Trail of Tears
Map Courtesy of the National Park Service

In the 1830's Native Americans of the southeastern United States were forcibly relocated west to Indian Territory (Oklahoma). The path of their relocation from their ancestral homes has been called **"The Trail of Tears."** Their passage through Arkansas took place over various old trails, including the Memphis-Fort Smith Road, the Cadron to Arkansas Post Road, and on the Arkansas River by steamboat.

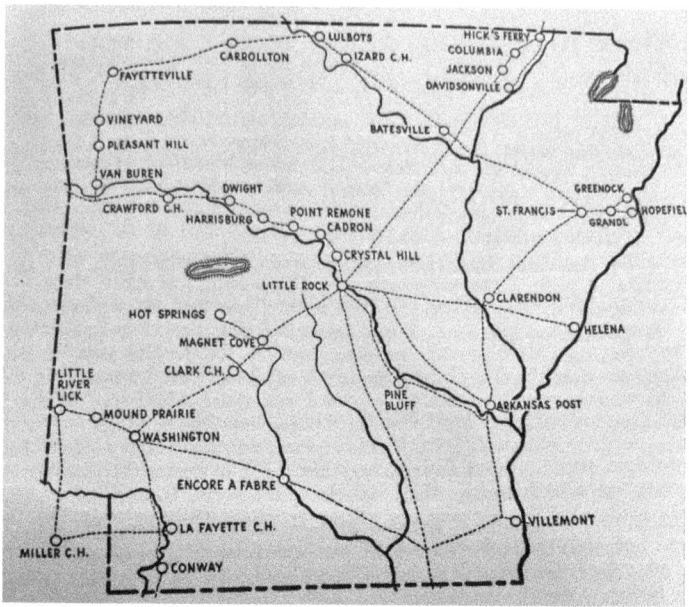

Arkansas Roads of 1836
The Arkansas Frontier, by Boyd Johnson, page 115-

In 1836, the year Arkansas became a state, this map by Boyd Johnson shows a growing web of trails reaching every corner of the new state. The muddy banks of numerous creeks and rivers still remained as major barriers to travel by wagon.

Many settlements cleared out a short road to the nearest navigable river. Major Stephen H. Long passed over some of the Arkansas roads in 1820, reporting, *"A few of the roads which traverse the country from the Mississippi to the upper settlements of the Red River and the Arkansas River have been sufficiently open to admit the passage of wagons."* He described the road between Little Rock and Hot Springs as *"an obscure path."* [The Arkansas Frontier, by Boyd Johnson, page 114]

In 1836, the first post road in Arkansas, built and maintained under contract with the Post Office for delivery of mail, was between Batesville and Lewisburg.

TYPES OF STAGES USED ON THE BUTTERFIELD OVERLAND NATIONAL HISTORIC TRAIL

Butterfield used two types of stages: a traditional "Mail Stagecoach" and a lighter weight "Celerity wagon." Both of these were ordered by John Butterfield from the J. S. & E. A. Abbot Co. of Concord, New Hampshire.

Shown below is the only existing image of a mail stagecoach used by Butterfield.

Basically lost for 120 years, this photo was re-discovered by Gerald T. Anhert in December 2023.

Mail Stagecoach Used by Butterfield
Daguerreotype image Courtesy of The Post-Standard, April 24, 1904, page 12 In Sept. 1858, commemorating the first trip of the Overland Mail Co. between St. Louis and San Francisco, this daguerreotype image was taken in front of Charles E. Butterfield's residence in Fayetteville, Arkansas.

John Butterfield Jr. is shown on the box, and A. B. Stafford holds the reins. Andrew Furlow stands at the head of the wheel horses. A second man, unnamed, standing near the rear wheel, may be passenger Waterman Ormsby. You can faintly see the lettering under the top railing: "Overland Mail Company."

Charles E. Butterfield's home as it appears today. This home, at 207 West Center Street, was rediscovered in Dec. 2023 by the research of Marilyn Heifner, president of THE BUTTERFIELD NATIONAL TRAILS Association. This "Walker-Stone" house is now the location of the Folk Art School of Fayetteville.

Photo by Marilyn Heifner **Charles Butterfield Home**

On rougher portions of the route, such as between Fayetteville and Fort Smith, and from Fort Smith to the California border, John Butterfield used a lighter weight stage called a "Celerity wagon" as shown below. Below is the only photograph in existence of a Butterfield owned Overland Mail Company Celerity wagon.

Celerity Wagon Used by Butterfield
The driver of the Celerity wagon shown above in the 'ten gallon hat' was David McLaughlin. This image was taken near the Cottonwood Stage Station, ElPaso, Texas. This copy of a 1861 daguerreotype image is courtesy of the Nita Stewart Haley Memorial Library at Midland, Texas.

This stagecoach in the Otero Museum, La Junta, Colorado was made by the same manufacturer as the Butterfield mail stagecoaches, Abbot-Downing, of Concord, New Hampshire.

Doug Hocking supplied this close up photo of No. 253 in the Otero Museum.

According to Gerald T. Ahnert, Butterfield authority and historian:

"Wells, Fargo & Company **never** operated on the Southern Overland Trail. They did operate as a stage company on the Central Overland Trail only from 1867 to 1869. They ordered 40 Concords for this purpose from Abbot-Downing, Concord, NH.

Today, only two of these 1858 original stagecoaches survive and the gear of a third. No. 251 is owned by the State of California and is on loan to the Wells Fargo History Museum, Old Town, San Diego, CA. The gear of coach No. 253, on which is hung the body of No. 106 is owned by Otero Museum in La Junta, Colorado. Pieces of coach No. 259 are exhibited at the Gateway Museum in St. Louis, Missouri. **All others represented in museums along the overland trails, and elsewhere, are replicas.**"

1866, Wagons Waiting at Argenta for the Ferry to Little Rock, Arkansas

WHAT ABOUT BUTTERFIELD'S STEAMBOAT?

On Aug. 2, 1858, six weeks before the first trip of the Overland Mail, John Butterfield wrote to his board of directors in New York. In part he wrote,

"With regard to the line from Memphis to Fort Smith I have deemed it prudent to wait and see what the condition of the river and the country would be when the late great floods shall have subsided their effects somewhat removed. Should the water prove to be too low in the Arkansas River a purchase of boats might prove injudicious. **I am of the opinion still (expressed in my former report) that the boats should be purchased at $7,500 each and run upon the Arkansas River. I think this will be the best method of doing our business and will be one of the best if not the very best paying portion of our entire route.** Negotiations are in progress for the purchase of boats and for the men to run them. Discretionary powers have been left with Mr. Crocker..." [For the full text of this letter, see pg 61 of Bob Crossman's book, "Butterfield Overland National Historic Trail PASSENGER DIARIES & STORIES Across Oklahoma, Arkansas, and Missouri, 1858 - 1861"]

Harper's Weekly Magazine, May 26, 1866, p. 328.

"Whipple Steamboat"
by David Garrison, Conte Crayon, November 19, 2010
Southeastern Community College, 1500 W. Agency Rd, West Burlington, Iowa

To John Butterfield's surprise, on about 8 occasions, was the Arkansas River at Pope and Conway Counties navigable between September of 1858 and March of 1861. On those 8 occasions John Butterfield was able to to employ his steamboat, the *Jennie Whipple*, to replace the stagecoaches and to carry mail and passengers from Fort Smith to Little Rock.

1866, "Big Rock on the Arkansas River"
Just a mile upstream from Little Rock is Big Rock
Source: Harper's Weekly Magazine, May 26, 1866, p. 328

According to the list of arrivals and departures printed in the *Arkansas Gazette* the dates the Jennie Whipple steamed between Fort Smith and Little Rock were: 1858 (Dec. 22nd to Fort Smith, 28th toward Little Rock, and 29th toward Fort Smith); 1859 (Jan. 3rd toward Little Rock, Jan 4th toward Fort Smith, and Jan. 8th toward Little Rock); 1860 (April toward Fort Smith, going aground upstream); and 1861 (April, finally unstuck and returned to Memphis).

1866, Arkansas River Port at Little Rock, Arkansas
From a sketch by James R. Taylor

On about 80 occasions, the water at Little Rock was navigable, allowing the Jennie Whipple to replace the stagecoaches between Little Rock and Memphis.

1861, Arkansas River Steamboat at Fort Smith & Van Buren
"Fort Smith, Arkansas, Recently Captured From the United States Secessionists," Illustrated London News, May 20, 1861, page 499

On all other occasions, the stations along the route received two eastbound and two westbound stagecoaches each week.

Combining stagecoach and steamboat trips, the Butterfield made a total of 520 trips through Faulkner County (260 westbound and 260 eastbound).

Ferry at Little Rock
1900 Photo of Ferry & Steamboat at Little Rock, Arkansas. At Little Rock, Butterfield's stagecoaches and steamboat each stopped, at the Butterfield Home Station- the Anthony House on Scott & Markham streets. The stagecoaches would then return to the ferry for a return trip across the Arkansas River to continue their journey. Photo Source: Images of America, Historic Pulaski County, by Paulette H. Walter and Alan C Paulson, page 41

Butterfield Overland National Historic Trail Through Arkansas' Pope & Conway Counties

Jennie Whipple
This is John Butterfield's steamboat, used on the
BUTTERFIELD OVERLAND NATIONAL HISTORIC TRAIL.
"Jennie Whipple" by artist Ralph Law. The original 24"x36" watercolor
and oil painting original is in the collection of Bob Crossman.

By Ralph Law (1927-1975) "One of the world's finest steamboat artists... executed in exacting detail after voluminous research. ...amazingly realistic steamboats from old postcards or photographs... with close attention to the smallest detail."
Quad-City Times, Davenport, Iowa, Feb. 18, 1975, page 1

In the fall of 1858, John Butterfield purchased the 1 year old steamboat, *Jennie Whipple*, in hopes of carrying the Overland Mail and passengers between Memphis and Fort Smith on the Arkansas River.

At the start, September 1858, the water depth of the Arkansas River was too low to reach Little Rock or Fort Smith.

Landing at Van Buren, "History Makers of Arkansas," 1918, by John Hugh Reynolds

—— The "Jennie Whipple," ——

"Long expected," has "come at last." She heralded her approach with the thundering echoes of a brass cannon stationed on her bow, a fine-toned church bell which she had on board, and strains of music from the Eau Claire Brass Band which went below on the St. Croix to meet her, last Friday.

—The Jennie Whipple is a queenly boat, and sits the water like a sea-gull.

The following are her dimensions:— Length, 138 ft.; breadth of beam, 30½ ft.; depth of hull, 3¾ ft.; length of main cabin, 55 ft.; length of ladies' cabin, 30 ft. She has 24 excellent state rooms, and her cabins are truly elegant, being finished and furnished in a style unsurpassed by that of any Mississippi boat. All in all, she is a model craft; and having been built exclusively for the Chippewa trade, Eau Clairians may well be proud of her. "Long may she *wave*." The officers of the 'Jennie Whipple" are gentlemen—every one of them, as we can conscientiously testify. Capt. WHIPPLE will ever be found ready to do the agreeable, and make his passengers comfortably at ease; while Mr. DONALDSON, the gentlemanly clerk, and "CHARLEY" GRAY, the mate, are not excelled in their respective stations. Of 1st Engineer WEST. CHURCH, we should say that he is eminently a handsome man, and can make the "Jennie" "Walk the waters like a thing of life."

Eau Claire Times, Eau Clarie, Wisconsin August 25, 1857

J. T. CHIDESTER

For years the literature on THE BUTTERFIELD OVERLAND NATIONAL HISTORIC TRAIL has contained only a brief mention of Butterfield's relationship with the Chidester stage line. For this reason, this extended chapter on that relationship is included here.

When it was time for the Overland Mail to begin in September, 1858, the summer drought and the extremely low water levels of the Arkansas River forced John Butterfield to avoid using his steamboat, the *Jennie Whipple*. He hurriedly contracted with an existing stage service – *Chidester, Reeside & Co.* – to provide passenger and mail service from Memphis to Fort Smith.

The McCollum – Chidester Home and Museum in Camden, Arkansas
Open Wed. to Sat., 9 - 4 for tours. Call 870-836-9243 to verify hours.

In the December 20, 2015 issue of the *Arkansas Gazette*, author Tom Dillard provided an excellent summary of Mr. Chidester:

"Butterfield, who knew little of the geography of Arkansas, assumed the stages departing St. Louis could travel due south through the Arkansas delta and connect with the Memphis stage, then proceed across mid-Arkansas to Fort Smith.

However, Butterfield soon learned that poor roads and vast swamps made it necessary for the St. Louis coaches to use a route through Springfield, Mo., and then travel through Northwest Arkansas to Fort Smith.

Again showing his unfamiliarity with the brutal realities of travel in frontier Arkansas, Butterfield assumed he could transport the mail from Memphis to Fort Smith via steamboat. However, low water levels made that approach impossible much of the time. Butterfield then contracted with Chidester's company to handle the Memphis-to-Fort Smith segment.

Chidester quickly set up a twice weekly route though he faced many obstacles. The slightest rains could turn delta roads into muddy quagmires. River transport was not reliable either.

Always innovative, Chidester drew upon a variety of options to get the mail across Arkansas. In addition to his fine Concord stage coaches, which had a capacity of 4,000 pounds, including nine passengers, Chidester relied upon existing railroads and steamboats to complete his appointed rounds...

As originally planned, the Overland Mail route ran due west from Memphis – which meant it passed about 25 miles north of the capital city. Mail from Little Rock was transported by buggy to the overland stop at Atlanta...

If rivers were sufficiently high to enable steamboat navigation, Butterfield owned vessels were pressed into service.

The Jenny Whipple plied the Arkansas between Little Rock and Fort Smith, while the Charm operated between Des Arc and Clarendon. The steamboats offered the advantages of a smooth ride, hot meals, and comfortable beds.

Chidester established a number of way stations and stops along the route to Fort Smith. From Des Arc the coaches journeyed along the north side of the Arkansas River through Cadron, Lewisburg (present-day Morrilton), Pottsville, and Norristown (modern Russellville) where the stage was ferried across the Arkansas River in order to complete the run to Fort Smith with stops at Dardanelle and Charleston among other places. [December 20, 2015 ,Arkansas Democrat Gazette, author Tom Dillard]

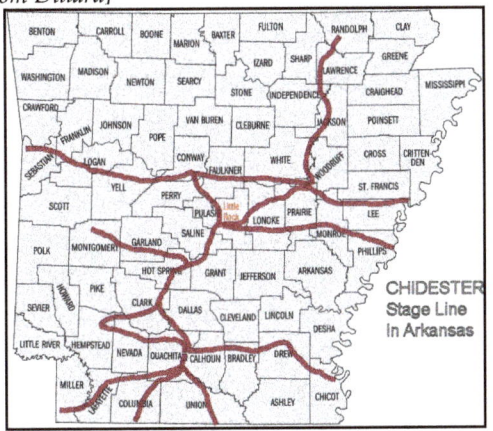

Chidester Stage Lines inArknasas
Map provided by the McCollum-Chidester Museum in Camden, Arkansas
Glendle Griggs, rgriggs@cablelynx.com

The map above shows the various stage routes that Chidester established - most of them before John Butterfield received the Overland Mail Co. contract.

While we usually credit John Butterfield for establishing the central Arkansas route, it may be more correct to credit John T. Chidester for setting the land stage route of home and swing stations between Memphis/Fort Smith in April of 1858.

Chidester Advertisement - Memphis to Little Rock in 26 to 30 Hours
The Chidester Operation was larger than just the Memphis-Fort Smith route as reflected in this advertisement in
The Memphis Daily Avalanche, issue of Jan. 22, 1859.

WHEN DID BUTTERFIELD'S SUB-CONTRACT WITH CHIDESTER END?

According to James Glover, Butterfield's Superintendent in Memphis, [*his letter reprinted in Feb. 9, 1859 issue of Arkansas True Democrat*]: From mid Sept. 1858 to about January 20, 1859, sub-contractor John T. Chidester, carried the Overland from Memphis to Fort Smith using Chidester owned stagecoaches, horses, and swing stations.

There were problems during the first four months. Memphis was learning by telegraph that the stages were arriving in St. Louis a day or so ahead of the stage bound for Memphis. Investigating the reason for the delays, Butterfield Agent Walton on Dec. 4, 1858, reported: *"owing to other contracts of the sub-contractors, the mail is laid over about 48 hours at Fort Smith, and about 24 at Des Arc. At present this can not be remedied."*

In Feb. 9, 1859, James Glover wrote, concerning these problems, that mostly due to poor road conditions and fulfilling their overlapping contract to carry the regular mail from Fort Smith to Memphis *"their route was so circuitous, and they had to stop at so many offices, that they were* unable to comply with this contract."

Therefore, a revised sub-contract was made between Butterfield and Chidester. The revised sub-contract, beginning about January 20, 1859, allowed Chidester 45 hours to carry the Overland Mail from Memphis to Dardanelle. At Dardanelle, the Overland Mail and passengers were transferred to Butterfield owned stages and horses for a 15-hour trip to Fort Smith, thereafter stopping at Butterfield operated swing stations between Dardanelle and Fort Smith. This new 60 hour plan would be 24 hours faster than the Fort Smith to St. Louis stage.

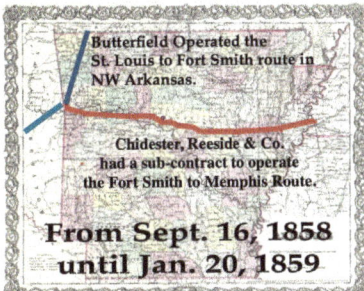 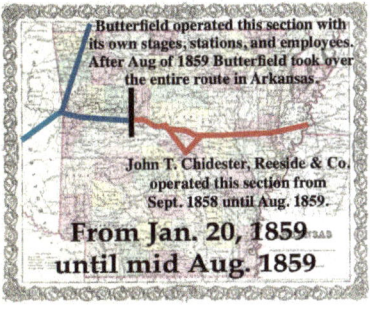

After August of 1859, giving up on the plan to use the steamboat Jennie Whipple between Fort Smith and Memphis, the Overland Mail Company ended their subcontract with Chidester, stocking the entire central Arkansas route with Butterfield owned stages, stations, horses and employees.

Butterfield's sub-contracting the Memphis to Fort Smith route to an existing mail carrier to John T. Chidester is the reason we have no exciting eyewitness accounts of the Overland's first arrival in Little Rock. In September 1858, nothing new was happening – John T. Chidester had been carrying the mail on this route already. The same mail coaches were driving over the same route, by the same drivers, and pulled by the same horses. **In many respects, between September 1858, and August 1859, the Memphis to Fort Smith route was a 'John T. Chidester' operation, not a 'John Butterfield' operation.**

Butterfield Overland National Historic Trail Through Arkansas' Pope & Conway Counties

What were the stations & ferries between Memphis and Fort Smith?

1. Post Office (Memphis, TN)

"1862 Memphis Post Office"

The 3,000 mile journey to San Francisco began at the Memphis Post Office where transcontinental mail bags were prepared for departure every Monday and Thursday at 8 am.

2. The Commercial Hotel (Memphis, TN)

Commercial Hotel

According to page two of the April 6, 1860 issue of the Memphis Daily Appeal, the Commercial Hotel housed Butterfield's Overland Mail offices in Memphis.

The hotel was built in 1848 and survived until about 1891. Departing the Memphis Post Office, the bags were transferred to the Butterfield offices at the Commercial Hotel, at the corner of Jefferson and Front Streets. From the hotel, mail and passengers were carried to the banks of the Mississippi River.

3. Steamboat *Jennie Whipple*

"The Jennie Whipple" *painted by Ralph Law.*
Original watercolor painting in the collection of Bob Crossman.

On about 80 occasions when the waters of the Arkansas River permitted, at the Memphis wharf mail and passengers boarded John Butterfield's steamboat Jennie Whipple to steam for Little Rock.

She steamed south on the Mississippi to the White River Cut-off, then up the Arkansas River toward Little Rock.

On about 4 round trips, the boat was able to go beyond Little Rock to reach Fort Smith. For most of 1860, the Jennie Whipple was stuck aground above Fort Smith.

4. The Mississippi River ferry, *Nashoba.*

Early Memphis to Hopefield Ferry, perhaps the ferry "Nashoba"
Image from Gene Gill, www.historic-memphis.com

On about 460 occasions at the Memphis wharf, the overland mail and passengers boarded the ferry Nashoba for a short ride across the Mississippi River to the opposite banks to board the train at the Hopefield, Arkansas depot.

The ferry Nashoba departed at 7:30 am. The Train left Hopefield at 8 a.m. arriving at Madison at 1:00 p.m. (Memphis Daily Avalanche, Oct. 26, 1858)

Concerning the ferry, the Tuesday, Feb. 8, 1859 issue of the Memphis Daily Avalanche reported: "CHANGE OF OWNERS - The former proprietors of the Memphis and Hopefield ferryboat Nashoba, have sold the boat and ferry privileges for a term of years to Messrs. Richardson and Everett, who have improved the boat, and rendered the line in many respects more efficient than heretofore."

5. The engine, "Little Rock"

Lettering on Coal Car: "M & L R R"
Source: Mike Hood, Civil Engineering Manager for the City of Little Rock

Departing the Hopefield depot, the overland mail and passengers enjoyed a short 24 mile trip to the end of the tracks. On most of this distance the track was elevated on trestle over the "great swamp" of eastern Arkansas.

The Nashville Union & American, Aug. 30, 1857 reported that the first steam engine of the 'Little Rock and Memphis Railroad' on this track out of Hopefield was the "Little Rock."

6. Twelve Miles East of Madison, Arkansas

1864 Map of Arkansas
The small arrow points to the end of the tracks in 1858,
where transfer was made to a light vehicle bound for Des Arc, Arkansas.

At the end of the tracks, 12 miles east of Madison, mail and passengers were transferred to a "light vehicle" for the 70 mile trip to Des Arc, Arkansas.

7. Oakland

1855 Map of Arkansas
showing old road from Madison to Des Arc
On the entire trail, swing stations averaged 15 miles apart. To traverse the 70 miles from tracks end to Des Arc, there was likely a swing station near Oakland for a change of fresh horses.

8. Cotton Plant

After Oakland, there was likely a swing station near Cotton Plant for another change of horses.

9. White River Ferry (Des Arc, AR)

White River Ferry at Des Arc
Image courtesy of White River Museum
To reach Des Arc, the Overland needed to cross the White River by Ferry

10. Jackson House (Des Arc, AR)

Jackson House Hotel

After crossing the White River by ferry, the Overland Mail Co. light vehicle arrived at the Jackson House Hotel, changing to a traditional Mail Stagecoach for the balance of the trip to Fort Smith.

The Jackson House was a 12 room structure located about 100 yards from the White River ferry landing. The stage office was in an attached 16 x 16 foot frame addition on the east side of the hotel.

The old Jackson Hotel, later known as the Des Arc Hotel, on 4th and Main in Des Arc, was demolished about 2011. Staff at the Des Arc Public Library and the Tax Assessors Office identify this image as the original structure used by Butterfield.

11. Hickory Plain

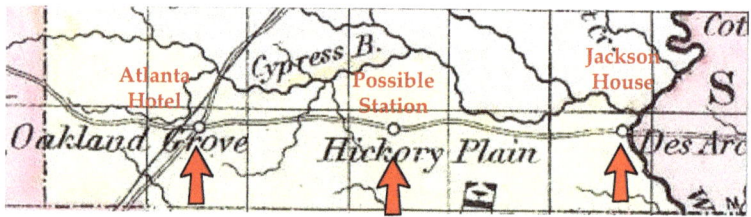

To traverse the 26 miles between Des Arc and Oakland Grove, there was likely a swing station at Hickory Plains for a change of fresh horses.

12. Atlanta Hotel (Oakland Grove, AR)

During the Butterfield years Oakland Grove had commercial establishments including a wool carding factory, cotton gin, sawmill, livery stable, two carriage shops, tailor shop, three doctors, saddle shop, two blacksmiths, grocery store, five dry goods stores, three saloons, and the Atlanta Hotel serving as the Butterfield Overland Mail Co. station.

"Witness Tree" ca. 1776

This tree 'witnessed' the Butterfield stagecoaches as they passed by.

This tree is ½ mile west of the Atlanta Hotel site. The tree is about 250 years old and has been measured and dated by a State Forester. It is listed among the Historical Trees of Arkansas. A pioneer cemetery with about 60 graves is within sight of this tree also.

Source: R. D. Keevern, Cabot, Arkansas. He taught history for 25 years at Jacksonville High School.

13. Gray Township Stage House (Jacksonville, AR)

Gray Stage House
Photo courtesy of Carolyn Kent

Halfway between the Atlanta Hotel and Little Rock, the stagecoach would have likely stopped at the 1830's Jacob Gray Stage House for a change of horses, according to historian Carolyn Kent.

14. Arkansas River Ferry (Argenta, AR)

The Old Ferry at Little Rock

Photo Source: Images of America, Historic Pulaski County, page 41
From Gray's Stage House to reach Little Rock, the stagecoach crossed the Arkansas River by ferry.

15. The Anthony House (Little Rock, AR)

The Anthony House

The stagecoach crossed on the ferry and stopped at the Anthony House at the southwest corner of Markham and Scott streets for mail and passengers.

Overland Office is at the Anthony House
Source: Weekly Arkansas Gazette, June 2, 1860

16. Palarm Creek Toll Bridge

The stage left the Anthony House and headed west to cross the toll bridge at Palarm Creek to enter Faulkner County.

17. Hartje's Tavern or Sevier's Tavern Swing Station

Sevier Tavern
This station was built by Robert Michael Sevier, and it served as a Butterfield swing station from 1860-1. This photo was taken about 1930.
Image Source: Faulkner County Museum, Lynita Langley-Ware, Director

Based on dates of construction, apparently the Hartje Tavern was the station in 1858 and 1859. The Sevier Tavern, built in 1860 served until 1861 as the station.

18. Cadron Ferry (Conway, AR)

To enter Conway County, the stage crossed Cadron Creek by ferry, just north of the Cadron Settlement. The property owner has shown author the location where a stage station was located on the Conway County side of the creek. This site appears to be too close to Hartjes and Plummers have been used by the Butterfield.

19. Plummer's Station (Plumerville, AR)

Plummer's Station, Photo by Bob Crossman in 2020
Samuel Plummer built this structure and adjacent leather shop about 1830.

20. Markham Tavern (Lewisburg, AR)

Markham Tavern
Rueben T. Markham built this tavern in 1832. It was relocated to Morrilton by James Moose about 1866. Photo courtesy of the Conway County History Museum

Entering Lewisburg, the stagecoach stopped at the Markham Tavern for fresh horses.

21. Hurricane Station (Atkins, AR)

Hurricane Station, *Photo by Bob Crossman in 2020*
Hurricane is located on the southeast side of present day Atkins.
Leaving Lewisburg, the stagecoach stopped at the Hurricane Station / Post Office, then on westward to Kirkbride Potts' Station.

22. Potts Station (Pottsville, AR)

Potts Station
Kirkbride Potts was the Butterfield Station Agent and the Postmaster.
Potts Station was built in 1858 by Kirkbride Potts, serving today as the Pope County Museum. Potts Station is still standing, and in excellent condition for its age.

Kirkbride Potts was the Butterfield Station Agent and the Postmaster.

Potts Station was built in 1858 by Kirkbride Potts, serving today as the Pope County Museum. Potts Station is still standing, and in excellent condition for its age.

23. Norristown Station & the Dardanelle Ferry

Cephas Washburn's old home was the Overland station at Norristown, according to Charles T. Davis' 1919 article in the Arkansas Gazette. This structure was nine miles west of Potts Inn Station. The Old Military Road crossed the Arkansas River at Dardanelle by ferry. Between January and August 1859, when Dardanelle was the terminus for Butterfield and Norristown was the terminus for Chidester Stage Line, there were most likely stations on both banks of the Arkansas River.

24. Stinnett's Swing Station

Site of Stinnett's Home Station
Historical marker is in center of photo.

Leaving the Dardanelle Ferry and Station, heading west the stage would arrive at Stinnett's Station. There is an historical marker near the site of the Stinnett Butterfield Swing Station on Hwy 22, along the lake, west of Dardanelle.

25. Shoal Creek Swing Station

This 1864 map shows the stagecoach road from Dardanelle Ferry to Shoal Creek

26. Creole Swing Station

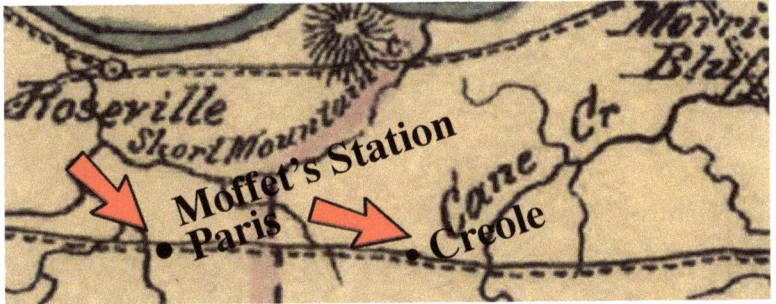

1864 Map showing old road between Creole and Paris

The Creole Station was one mile northwest of Subiaco, Arkansas on the 1827 Old Military Road.

27. Moffet's Home Station (northeast of Paris, AR)

Moffett's Station is thought to have been near this site.

This is a 2021 photo of the land southwest of the intersection of Kalamazoo Road and Old Military Road, northeast of Paris, Arkansas.

28. A. J. Singleton's Station (Charleston, AR)

Singleton's Station *showing the rear side. At the time of the Butterfield there was a kitchen addition on this side of the house.*
Image Source: Charleston Express, July 9, 1976

At Charleston, Arkansas, the A. J. Singleton Station was built in late 1850 for the stage coach. The property passed on to the Cormack family who were still the property owners when this photograph was taken in 1976.

29. Strang Station (Lavaca, AR)

The lower arrow is pointing to all that remains of the Strang Station used by the Butterfield – the old well.

30. Barling Station

The stage may have also stopped at Barling, halfway to Fort Smith, at the 1819 Mercantile store started by Aaron Barling.

31. Roger's City Hotel at Fort Smith, AR

John Roger's City Hotel
The Overland offices were here. Also, the employees of the Butterfield boarded here and Stables were located to the rear for 100 horses.
From here stages headed west to San Francisco.

32. St. Charles Hotel at Fort Smith, AR

St Charles Hotel
After the City Hotel burned Sept. 1860, offices of the Butterfield were moved to the St. Charles Hotel about a block to the north.

Leaving Fort Smith, the stages entered Indian Territory (Oklahoma), Texas, New Mexico, Arizona, Mexico, and California reaching their final destination at San Francisco in a total of 25 days or less.

The Butterfield Overland Historic National Trail through Missouri, Arkansas and Oklahoma:

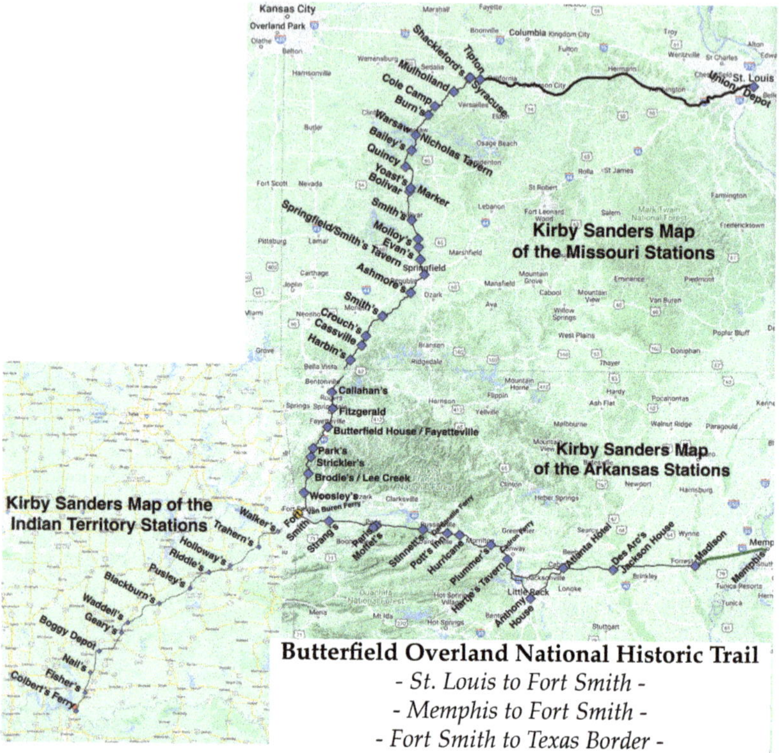

Kirby Sanders Map of the Missouri Stations

Kirby Sanders Map of the Arkansas Stations

Kirby Sanders Map of the Indian Territory Stations

Butterfield Overland National Historic Trail
- St. Louis to Fort Smith -
- Memphis to Fort Smith -
- Fort Smith to Texas Border -
Image Source: Kirby Sanders

The Butterfield Overland Historic National Trail - twice a week in 25 days or less:

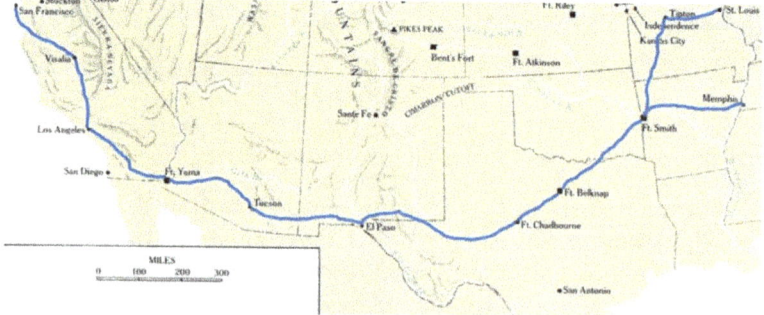

Map courtesy of Richard Frajola, "The Routes" page 3

Butterfield Overland National Historic Trail Through Arkansas' Pope & Conway Counties

BUTTERFIELD OVERLAND NATIONAL HISTORIC TRAIL THROUGH CONWAY COUNTY, ARKANSAS

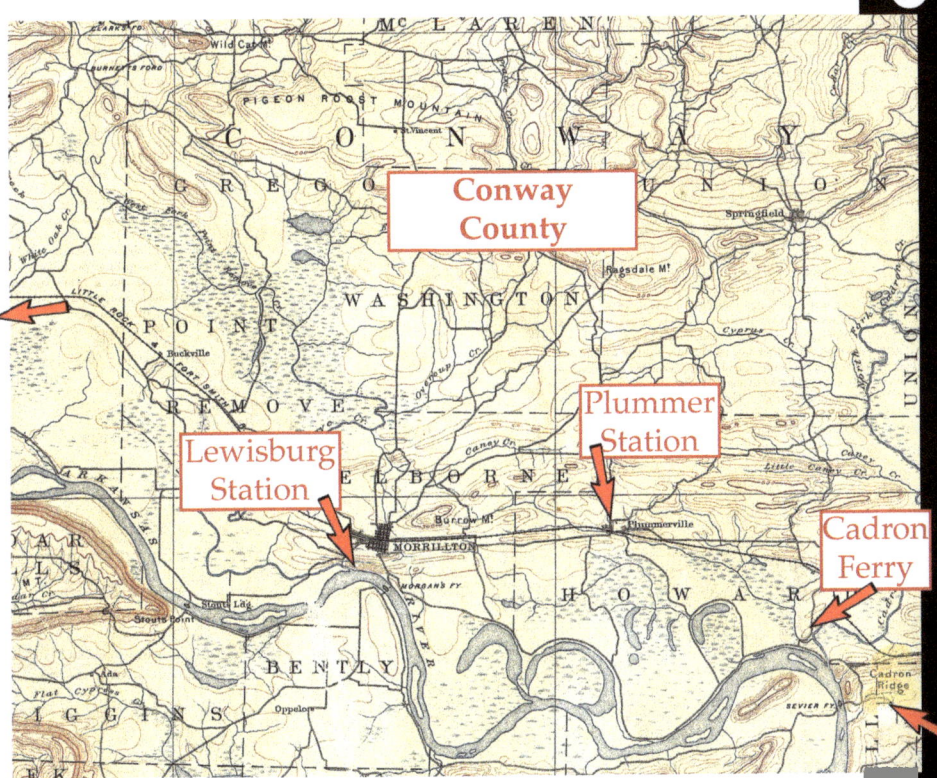

1888 Topographical Map, *USGS, Henry Gannett chief geographer, topography by H. B. Blair from 1888 survey.*

1894 USGS Topographical Map, Conway County, Arkansas

Butterfield Overland National Historic Trail Through Arkansas' Pope & Conway Counties

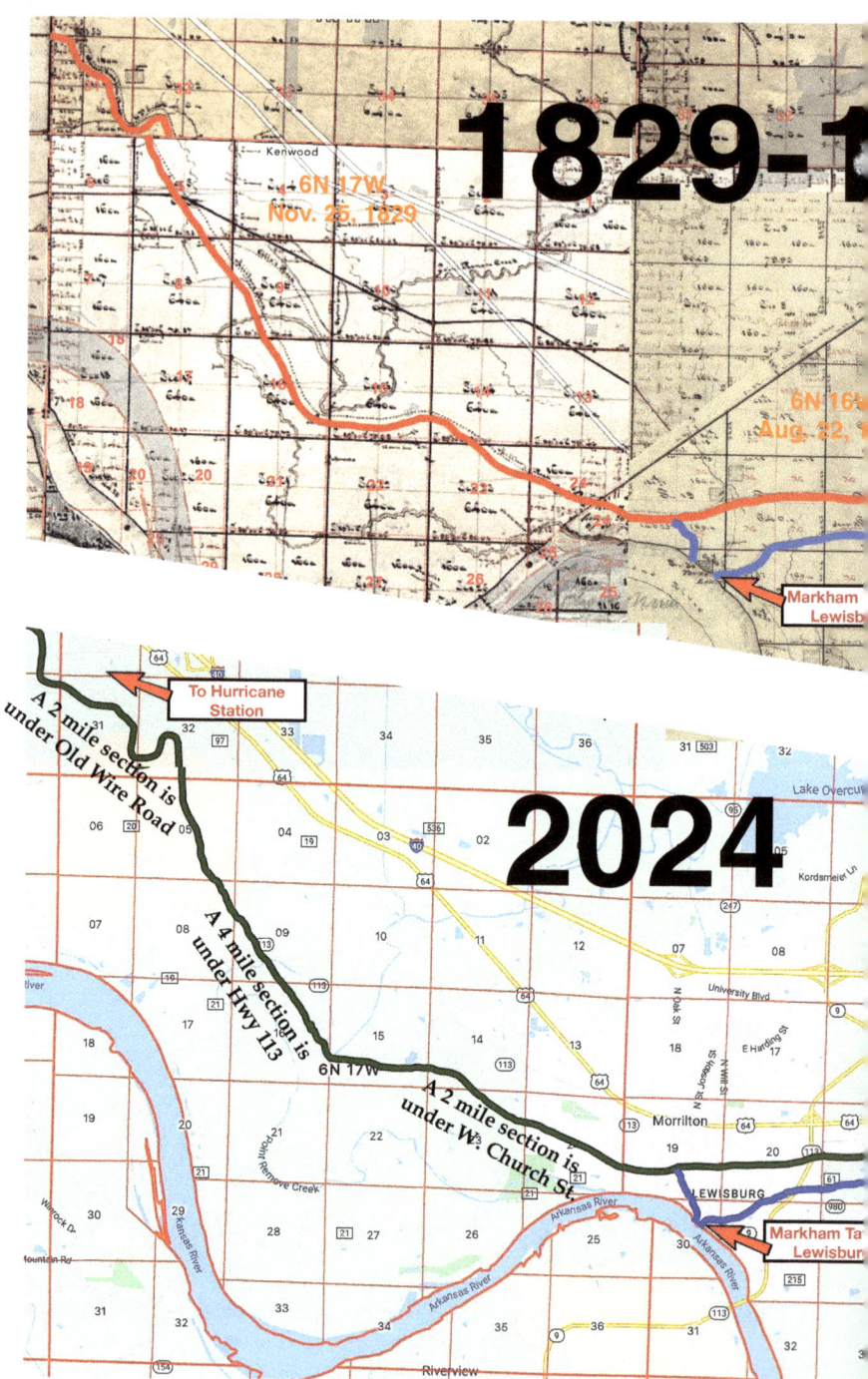

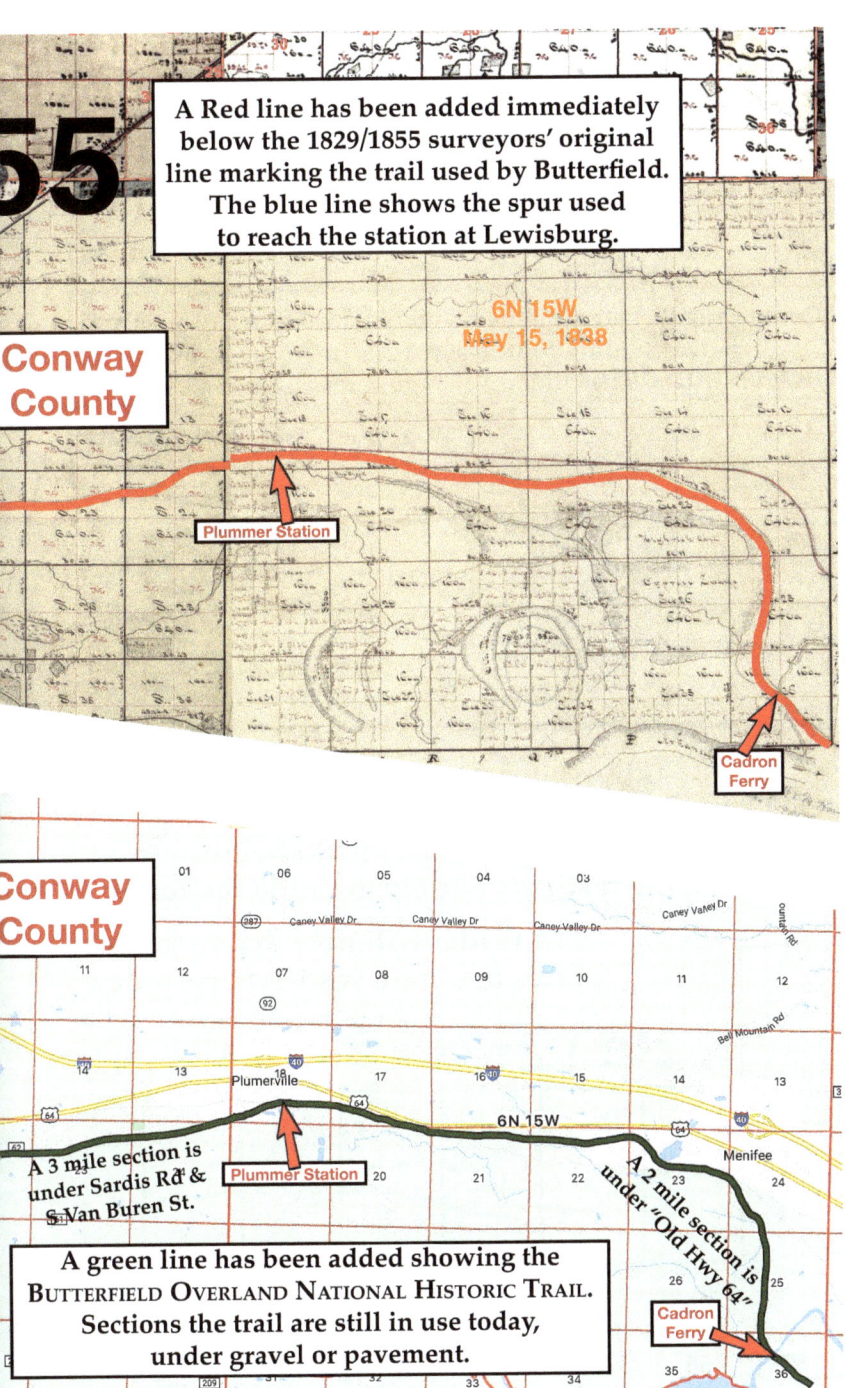

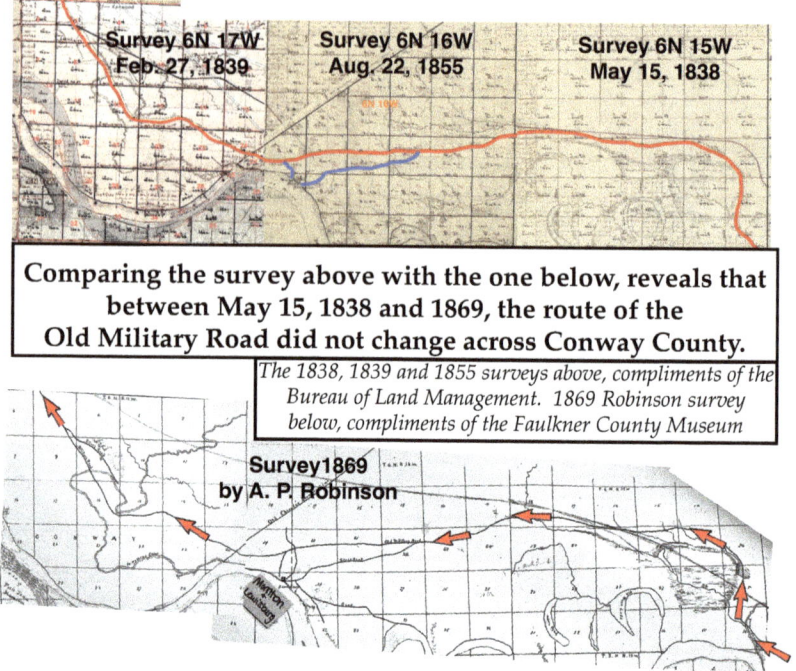

Comparing the survey above with the one below, reveals that between May 15, 1838 and 1869, the route of the Old Military Road did not change across Conway County.

The 1838, 1839 and 1855 surveys above, compliments of the Bureau of Land Management. 1869 Robinson survey below, compliments of the Faulkner County Museum

On the following 8 pages, the route through Conway County has been greatly enlarged. They piece together as shown below, allowing the reader to closely examine the route.

The reader will note that in many places the route is still in use today.

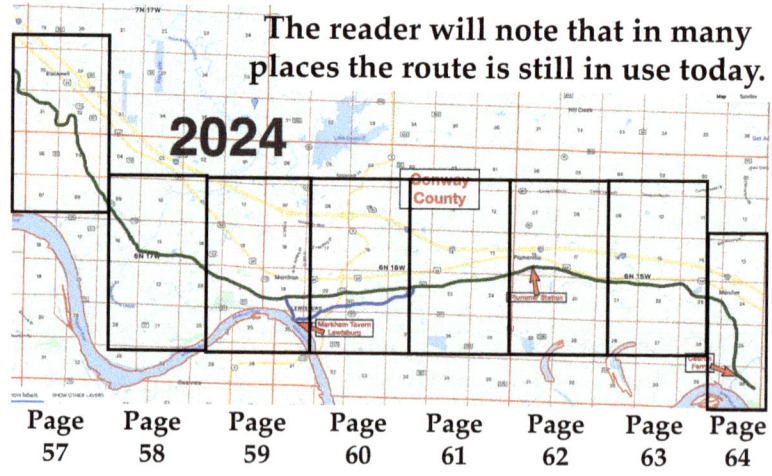

| Page 57 | Page 58 | Page 59 | Page 60 | Page 61 | Page 62 | Page 63 | Page 64 |

Butterfield Overland National Historic Trail Through Arkansas' Pope & Conway Counties

Butterfield Overland National Historic Trail Through Arkansas' Pope & Conway Counties

Butterfield Overland National Historic Trail Through Arkansas' Pope & Conway Counties

Butterfield Overland National Historic Trail Through Arkansas' Pope & Conway Counties

Butterfield Overland National Historic Trail Through Arkansas' Pope & Conway Counties

Butterfield Overland National Historic Trail Through Arkansas' Pope & Conway Counties

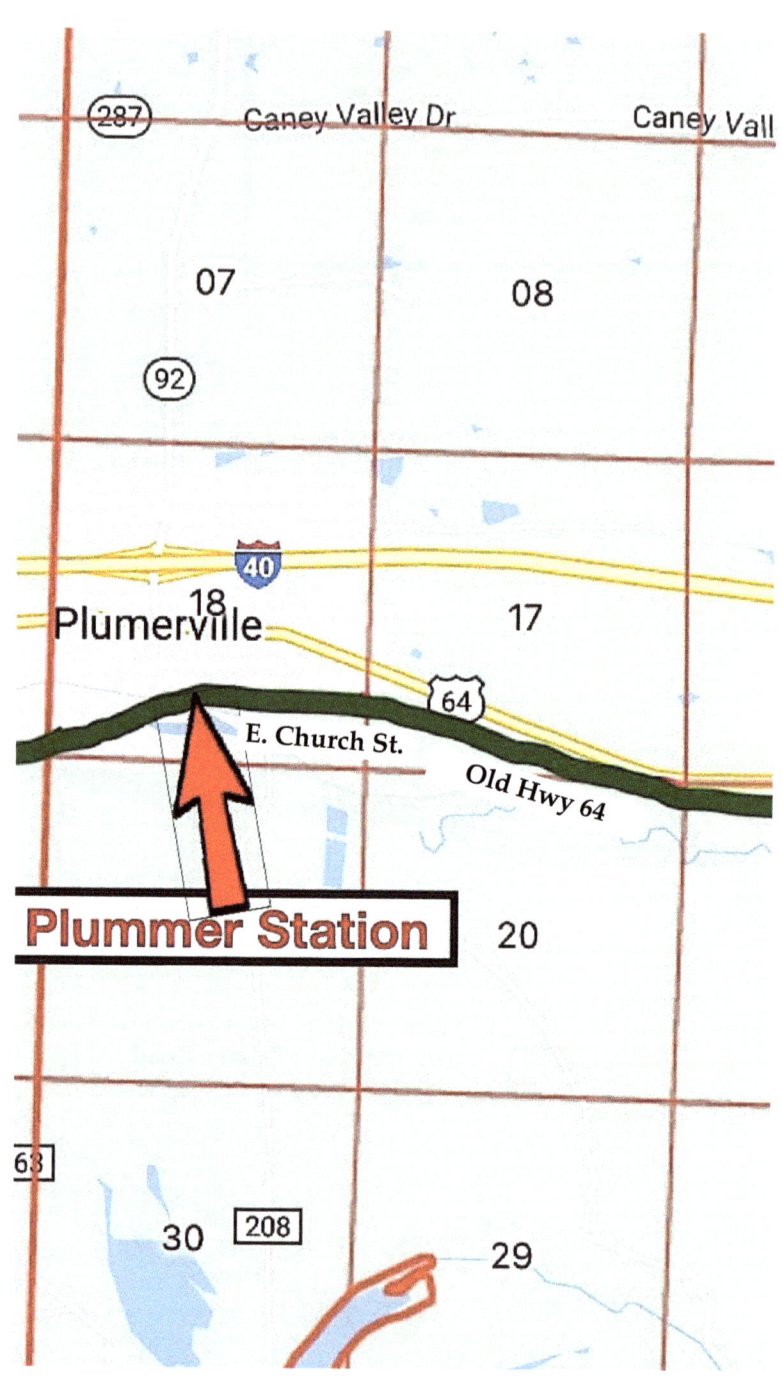

Butterfield Overland National Historic Trail Through Arkansas' Pope & Conway Counties

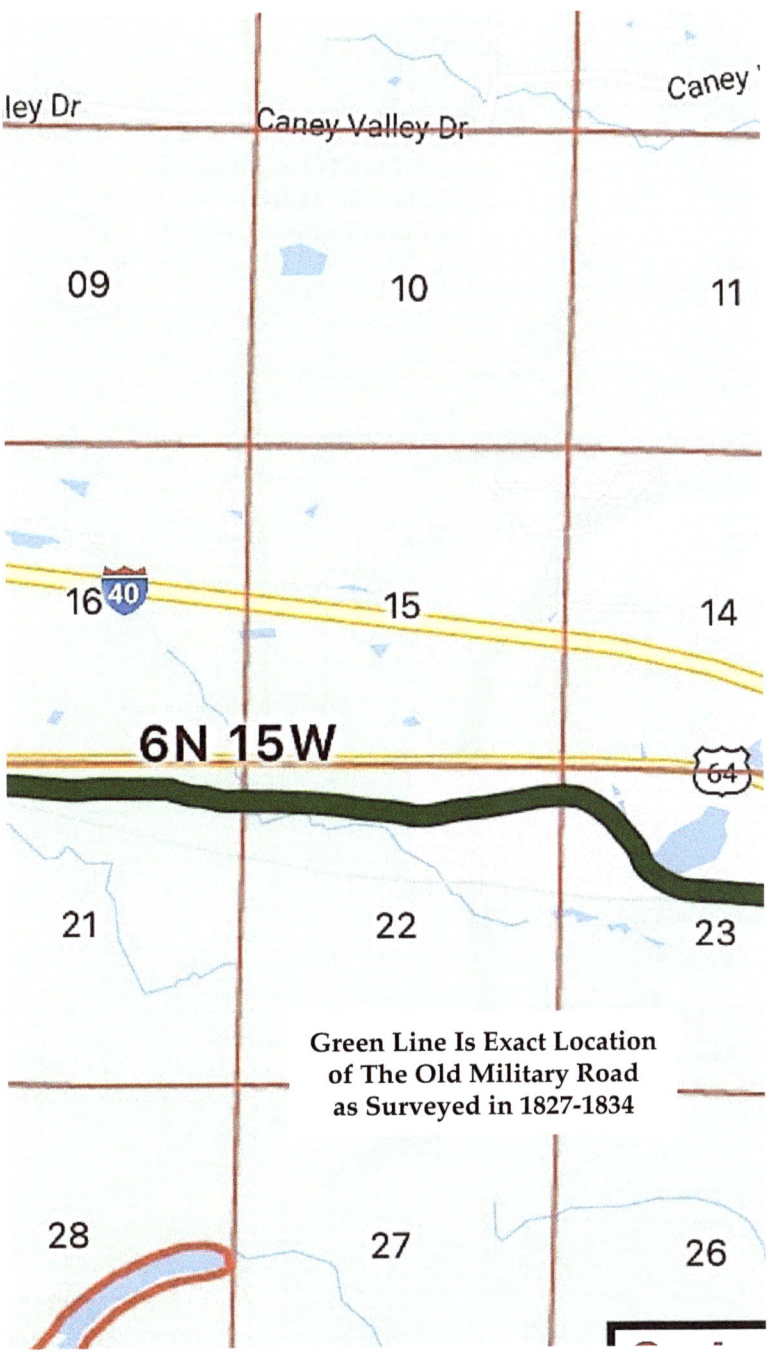

Green Line Is Exact Location of The Old Military Road as Surveyed in 1827-1834

Butterfield Overland National Historic Trail Through Arkansas' Pope & Conway Counties

Butterfield Overland National Historic Trail Through Arkansas' Pope & Conway Counties

"I have so much to tend to it is out of my power. I have to work in the shop and in the farm and tend to travelers on the road. It is impossible tho I am glad..."

Source: Samuel Plummer letter, Oct. 3, 1853

Discovery of Samuel Plummer's Station
N 35.156139, W -92.642917

After departing Memphis every Monday and Thursday morning at 8am, about 45 hours later the Butterfield Overland Mail Company stagecoaches heading westbound stopped at the Anthony Hotel in Little Rock. Leaving the hotel the stage crossed the Arkansas River by ferry and headed west along the north bank of the river. Reaching the Faulkner County line, the stage crossed the toll bridge at Palarm Creek, stopping at the Hartje or Sevier Tavern before entering Conway County at Cadron Creek.

Butterfield's Overland crossed Cadron Creek by ferry near this location.
"The Butterfield Overland Mail Route Through Faulkner County," by D. Brooks Green and David A. Dempsey, Faulkner Facts and Fiddlings, Faulkner County Historical Society, Vol. 24, Spring & Summer 1982, p.13-20

Crossing on the Cadron Ferry, the stage continued west to Plummer's Station, Lewisburg, Hurricane, Potts Inn, Norristown's Dardanelle Ferry crossing and on toward Fort Smith.

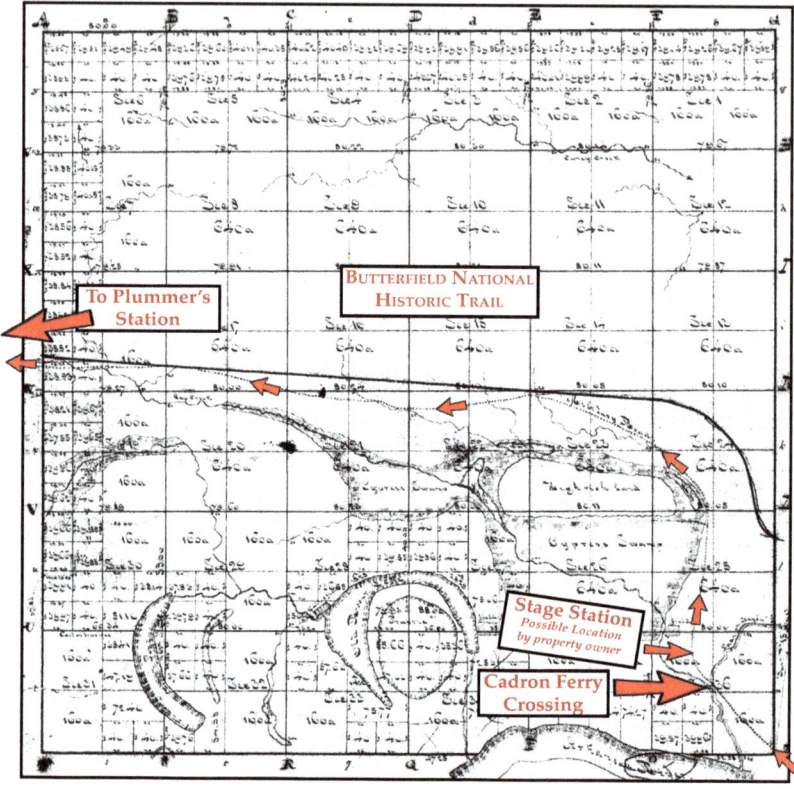

Detail survey of the trail from Cadron to Plummers, 1837
Surveyor Public Lands Office, Little Rock 15 May 1838
The above Plat of Township 6 North Range 15 West of the 5th Principal Meridian is strictly conformable to the field notes of the Survey thereof on file in this office which have been examined & approved. The East and South boundaries were surveyed in January 1819 by Wm H. Paltis D. S. The subdivision and meanders amounting to 68 miles 56 05/100 chains were surveyed in July 1837 by Thomas Mathers D. S. under instructions of the 23rd June 1837. Payment for the subdivision & meanders was made by Edward Cross Surveyor Public Lands & Charged in the accounts of the 3rd quarter of 1837. Voucher at 8Sum of all the actions set down on the above plate 22239.93 Edward Cross Surveyor Public Land

We have no description of the Cadron Ferry, but the South Dakota image below is typical of a simple flat bottom ferry of the 1850's in common use across Arkansas.

Example of Typical Flat Bottom Ferry

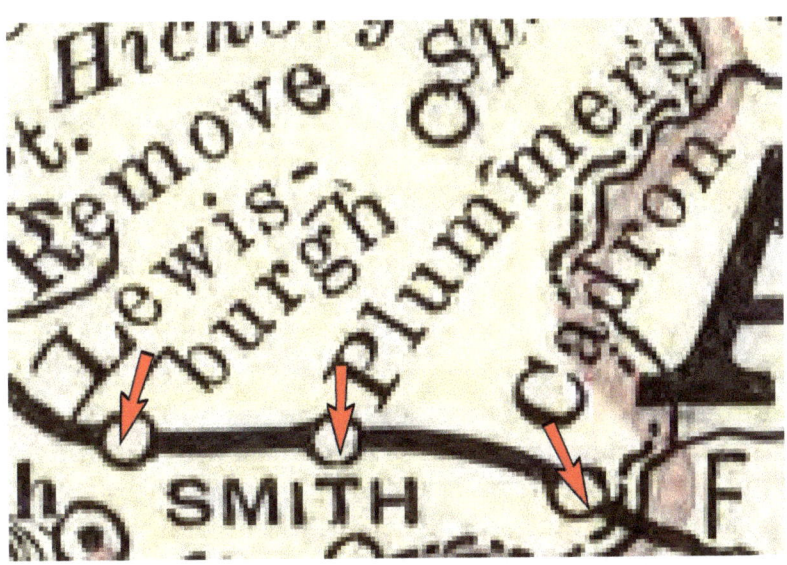

1881 map showing Cadron Ferry, Plummer's and Lewisburg. along the trail used by Butterfield's stagecoaches.

Crossing at Cadron Ferry, the westbound Butterfield's Overland Mail Company stagecoach next stopped at Plummer's Station, where Samuel Plummer was the station agent. The community that arose around the station is now called Plumerville.

Samuel Plummer

Samuel Plummer was born at Washington, D. C. in 1801 and died at age 75 in Conway County on February 4, 1876. He is buried in a family cemetery on a slight bluff along the north side of the railroad tracks. His wife preceded him in death by 31 years, on October 6, 1845 at age 39. Together they had five sons and five daughters.

Plummer Family Cemetery
Across the railroad, northeast of the Plummer Station

Samuel Plummer, orphaned at 7, was taken in and reared by Partick Rogers, a saddler who taught his young charge the leather trade. Plummer moved from Washington DC to Boston about 1824, where he worked for the leather goods company, Foster and Barton. A year later he decided to move west, and in the company of Maj. Edward W. Duval, an Indian Agent to the Cherokees. He arrived in Arkansas in 1825.

Plummer married Henrietta Ellis of Pope County March 25, 1828 and the couple settled in Lewisburg.

On May 30, 1828, Samuel Plummer paid $100 to

George Harris for 160 acres along Gap Creek, where Plummer's station would eventually be located. At the time of purchase the land along Gap Creek was planted with fruit trees and a cabin. The existing 14' x 14' log cabin was enlarged by the addition of an attached Leather Shop. In the 1850 and 1860 census Samuel's occupation is listed as "Saddler."

About 1900 the log cabin was covered with wood siding, and the interior walls were covered with plank boards. The building was standing, although in poor condition, until December 2022. In 2023, after an accidental fire, the city completely hauled off the burnt remains of the station, leaving the leather shop.

The address where the cabin once stood is 301 S. Van Buren Street, Plumerville, Arkansas

Henrietta Plummer brought several enslaved persons with her. She supervised their work clearing and cultivating all of the tillable land they had purchased. According to the 1830 census, she had 2 enslaved males under the age of ten, and 1 male enslaved between the ages of 36 and 54, totaling three enslaved.

Living on the Old Military Road, also known today as the Trail of Tears, Samuel Plummer sold leather goods to the Cherokees who camped south of his property as they were being forcefully relocated to Indian Territory. From 1858 to 1861 his leather shop serviced the Butterfield stagecoaches, and during the Civil War he sold saddles and other leather goods to the Confederate Army.

The community that grew up around Samuel Plummer's homestead came to consider him the founder of the community. The town was also named Plummerville with two 'm's like the founder. At some point, an 'm' was dropped, so the town is now called Plumerville with one 'm.'

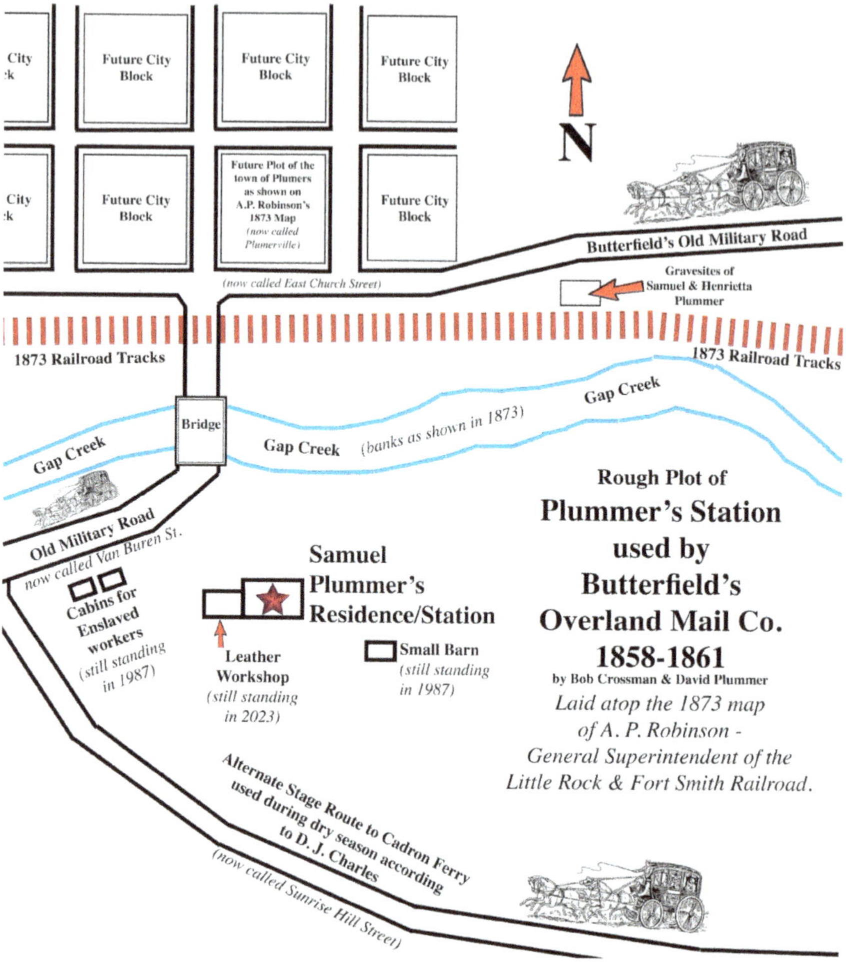

Butterfield Overland National Historic Trail Through Arkansas' Pope & Conway Counties

Rough Plot of Plummer's Station used by Butterfield's Overland Mail Co. 1858-1861
by Bob Crossman & David Plummer

Laid atop the 1873 map of A. P. Robinson - General Superintendent of the Little Rock & Fort Smith Railroad.

This is a closeup of the 1889 USGA topographical map by Henry Gannett. This clearly shows a jog in the old Military Road where it crossed the creek in front of Samuel Plummer's Station.

© 2024 Robert O. Crossman

Plummer's Station as it appeared about 1950.
About 1900, this log house's exterior was covered with wood siding.

This barn at Plummer's Station, was still standing in 1987

The letter below was written by Patrick Rogers to Samuel Plummer on Sept. 30, 1824 while Samuel still lived in Washington DC.

Dear Friend

Your two letters arrived in due time by your last received this day. I am happy to hear that your health is improving and that you have got a good situation. You will no doubt learn many things in your business by seeing the different methods of doing work a lesson on, that takes notice of the various methods in which work is done will be improved very much by taking advantage of every circumstance in which his knowledge may be improved. I hope we shall see you in Washington before the cold weather sets in & that you will bring with you a fund of Yankee notions treasured up in your mind to instruct & entertain all your friends in this part of the country. You will oblige me by making inquiry how trunk boards maybe had in Boston. I should like to procure about 4 or 5 hundred wt If you can make any arrangement to that Effect, either by a draft on me or delivery at Washington or in any other way that it can be done. Mr. Bell & family are all well & desire to be kindly remembered to you. Mr. Craydock and family of Mr. Davis & family likewise join in their best wishes for your welfare. In the form of news I have little to say that is very pleasing this morning we have this morning lost our Mayor which is considered a general loss. His death is much lamented. Before this reaches you he will be numbered with his father. Mr. Pack our neighbor has also been carried to his long home. Our City generally speaking is healthy for this season of the year but there is some sickness ___ _____ has had a slight attack of _____ but is on the _____. All with us have been blessed so far with health. Our neighbors generally, healthy, all your friends are happy to hear that you are doing well. Sisters _____ to be remembered to you & from me in their best wishes for your welfare.

I remain sincerely yours,
Patrick Rogers

PS I accidentally heard that _____ was in New York, which surprised me very much. If you come through New York you may probably see him if you come through New York. ____ ___ a ___ ___ ___ you would call on my Brother John you will find him at No. 127 Broadway, New York. I had almost forgot Mr. ____ tell him Sisters of Mr. _____ to remember to him PR

The document below is a real estate transaction between Samuel Plummer and George Harris, May 30, 1828.

Know all men by these Presents that I George Harris claim the one half of the South West Quarter of Section eighteen Township Six North of Range fifteen West and have sold the same to Samuel Plumer. Now therefore be it known that I hereby for the consideration of one hundred dollars paid me by said Plumer agree & covenant to convey to said Plumer and his heirs by Warranty Deed in fee simple estate in _____ the one half of said quarter section of land that shall as may be entered in my name. And said Plumer buying the government _____ _____ land unto the Land Office. Witness my hand and seal this 30th May, 1828.

George Harris

Witness
Chester
Ashly & __
Brown

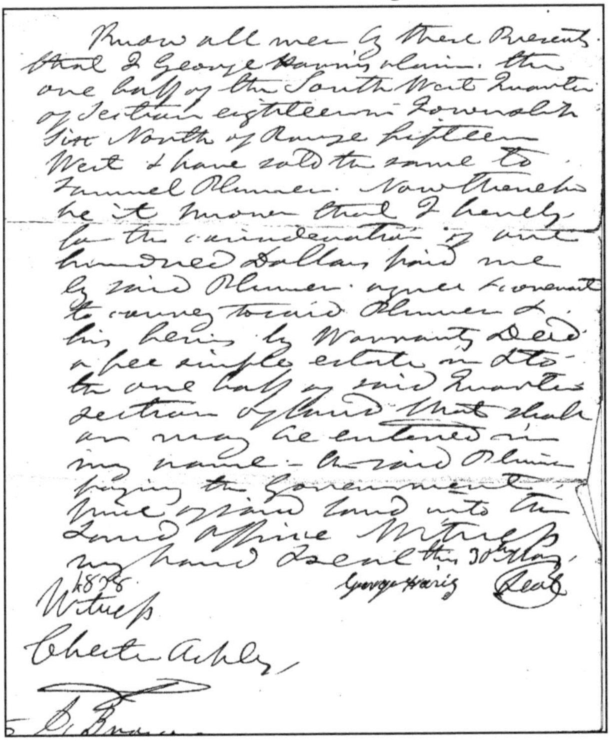

This sale was not registered until March 27, 1833 (see following document).

**Deed of Sale
March 27, 1833
Samuel Plummer purchased from George Harris**

This indenture made and entered into this 27th day of March in the Year of our Lord One thousand eight hundred & thirty three by & Between George Harris of the County of Conway & Territory of Arkansas of the one part, and Samuel Plummer of the same place of the other Part:

Witnesseth: that the said George Harris for and in consideration of the sum of one hundred Dollars to him in hand paid the receipt Whereof is hereby acknowledged, hath this day bargained granted sold & confirms unto the said Samuel Plummer this heirs & assigns forever, and by these presents do hereby bargain grant sell assign & confirm unto the said Samuel Plummer his heirs & assigns forever, my improvements on Gap Creek in the County & Territory aforesaid & the same one which I now live, including my Cabins, fruit trees, cleared land and all the appurtenances, privileges, thereunto belonging or in anywise appertaining with any right to preemption of the same, to have and to hold the same unto him the said Samuel Plummer his heirs & assigns forever & hereby warrant & forever defend the same to the said Samuel Plummer against myself and heirs and against every person claiming under myself, my heirs & In testimony whereof I have here unto set my hand affixed my seal this day and date above written. Signed sealed & delivered ...

Now on this day appeared Before me the under signed an acting Justice of the Peace for the County & State afore said George Harris and acknowledged to the above and for going instrument of writing to be his act and deed for the purpose is there in mentioned and contained given under my hand and seal this 28th day of September 1837.

E. W. Owens JP

**Samuel Plummer
(1800-1879)
Station Agent of
Plummer's Station**
Samuel sometimes signed his name with only one "m."

Courtesy of David Plummer

"I have so much to tend to it is out of my power. I have to work in the shop and in the farm and tend to travelers on the road. It is impossible tho I am glad..."

Source: Samuel Plummer letter to his daughters, Oct. 3, 1853

In 2014 David Plummer is pictured here standing by the recently restored grave sites of Samuel & Henrietta Plummer.

Samuel was the operator of the Plummer's Swing Station used by Butterfield's Overland, 1858-1861.

Photo by David Plummer

Plummer's Station and Leather Shop ca. 1950

The original cabin was a single room that measured 14 by 14 feet, with a fireplace. In the next decade, Plummer added an open breezeway and a second log room to house his leather shop. In time, a series of wood frame rooms were added on the rear to help accommodate Plummer's large family, his saddlery and the stagecoach stop that the cabin eventually became. About 1900, the house was covered with siding and reroofed, the interior covered with plank boards and the breezeway enclosed to make a hallway.

The south side of Plummer's Station ca. 1950

This enslaved workers cabin at Plummer Station was still standing in 1987
In the 1830's, living at Samuel Plummer's were 2 enslaved males under the age of ten, and 1 enslaved male between the ages of 36 and 54, totaling three enslaved.

This enslaved workers cabin at Plummers Station was still standing in 1987.

Plummer's Station and leather shop as it appeared in 2020 Before the Fire
"Preserve Arkansas, 2020 Most Endangered Places Spotlight: Plummer's Station," May 24, 2020,
www.facebook.com/PreserveAR/posts/10158244201504356

Plummer's Station After the Fire of 2023, Leather Shop Still Standing
According to the family, the station was noted for its excellent meals and it became a place where the passengers would choose to lodge a night or two, catching the next stage through to their destination.
Photo by Bob Crossman December 2023

Leather Shop at Plummers Station
After the fire of 2023 the station's structure was removed, leaving Samuel Plummers Leather Shop standing alone.
Photo by Bob Crossman June 2024

East Side of Leather Shop at Plummers Station
This shows the east side of the Leather Shop where it connected to the 1830 Station structure.
Photo by Bob Crossman June 2024

Attic Boards of Leather Shop
Closeup of east side with station removed. *Photo by Bob Crossman June 2024*

Foundation of Leather Shop
Closeup of southeast corner. *Photo by Bob Crossman June '24*

Gap Creek Flows In Front of Plummers Station
Photo by Bob Crossman June 2024 from the bridge looking east.

In this early street scene of Plumerville, the Peel Hotel is on the left, and A. R. Bowdre's Dry Goods Store is on the right.

This is the bridge of the Butterfield Trail crossing Gap Creek, connecting Plummer's Station with the town.
Note the Peel Hotel on left across the bridge.

The two oldest children of Samuel and Henrietta were Mary Jain and Ann Eliza. They married brothers Hiram and David Perry Allen. In 1852, Mary Jain and Ann Eliza, along with their husbands left Arkansas on a wagon train bound for California following the Cherokee Trail. The first child of Mary Jain and Hiram, William, died during the journey in southern Wyoming. Miraculously, William's gravesite was discovered in the late 1900's and is now surrounded by a protective enclosure.

Samuel Plummer's Feb. 4, 1876 obituary reads,
"On the 21st instant at his residence in this county, Samuel Plummer, aged about 75 years. Mr. Plummer was one of the pioneers of the county, and perhaps been continuously resident longer than any other man in it. Only by the links are sundered that bind us to the past.

In old days of primitive mode of travel, Plummer's was a noted stand as was the Palarm, the Cadron, Point Remove, Lewis' and Potts.' And, of all those worthy roadside landlords who gave cheer and needed rest to the weary traveler, none remain but Mr. Potts.

We have not been able to gather the particular incidents of Mr. Plummer's death further than that he was going about in the morning and attending to business as usual, suddenly complained of feeling unwell, lay down and died before serious danger was apprehended. We know not another left who can tell us of the incidents of 40 years ago.

Would it not be well for the sons of the pioneers to write out for publication, incidents in their father's lives? We should be pleased to institute the 'Pioneers Column,' which should be weekly filled by loving and honest hands with sketches of our early history."

Another death notice reads: *Mr. Samuel Plummer, an old citizen at Plummer Station, Conway County, died* at his home... He was known by hundreds of Arkansans, all of whom remember him as a happy, genial, whole-souled farmer. His house was for years the stage stand on the old Little Rock and Fort Smith stage road. His death is greatly lamented. (Daily Arkansas Gazette, Feb. 23, 1876, page 4)

The Pope County paper added: *"It will cast a shade of sorrow over many, and many an auld lang syne acquaintance of Samuel Plummer to learn that the genial old pioneer has forever quit the walks of men and had his ashes fathered unto his fathers."* (Russellville Democrat, March 2, 1876, p.1)

Plumerville as seen from the hills south of town.

Homer Bradley's Barber Shop at Plumerville
This is a great image of the typical 1900 wooden structure for small businesses in Arkansas. They were not built on concrete slabs, rather the structure sits atop native rock foundation walls.

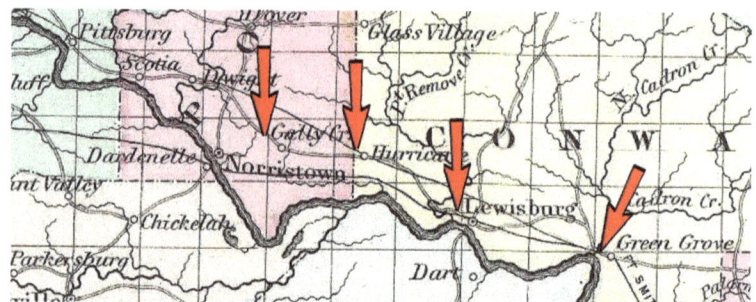

This 1855 Map showing the old stagecoach road between Cadron, Lewisburg, Hurricane and Gally Creek .
1855 Map of Arkansas, Published by J.H. Colton & Co., New York

The 7 Hour Delay at Plummer's Station?

The route from Memphis to Little Rock continued to prove problematic, along with excessive rains turning the roads through the eastern swamps into quagmire. This was evident in mid-February 1859, when Texas Ranger Major Ben McCullough traveled from Fort Smith to Memphis. He reported that the route still had problems, and it was his impression that there was a Yankee plot to kill the Memphis branch by making service intolerable.

The Weekly Arkansas Gazette reported:

*"Maj. McCullough informs us, further, that instead of being forwarded by the stages of Butterfield & Co. immediately, as were the St. Louis passengers, the Arkansas and Memphis passengers were detained at Fort Smith from twelve till half past three o'clock; and on the route, that they were detained at Dardanelle from eight o'clock in the forenoon until one o'clock in the afternoon; than they were **detained at Mr. Plummer's in Conway County, from ten o'clock at night until five o'clock next morning.** It took the stages from five o'clock in the morning until six o'clock in the evening to reach Little Rock – a distance of only forty-three miles; and they were detained at Little Rock from six o'clock Saturday eve-*

ning until the next Monday at four o'clock in the morning - making, in all a detention of more than forty-eight hours from the time of the arrival of the stages at Fort Smith, until their departure from Little Rock for Memphis." *Weekly Arkansas Gazette, Little Rock, Arkansas, Sat., Feb. 19, 1859*

To better understand Major McCullough's complaints, we need to explore the contract between Butterfield and the Chidester stage line.

As discussed at length earlier in this book, starting about January 20, 1859, Butterfield employees were given only 15 hours to make the trip from Fort Smith to Dardanelle. At Dardanelle, mail and passengers were transferred to the Chidester stage line. Chidester was given only 45 hours to carry the Overland from Dardanelle to Memphis.

So, Major McCullough's trip from Fort Smith to Memphis occurred in the first month of this new arrangement and it is obvious the Chidester stage line did not get the Major to Memphis in 45 hours. Rather, the Major was delayed 5 hours at Dardanelle, 7 hours at Plummer's and 34 hours at Little Rock in Chidester stagecoaches.

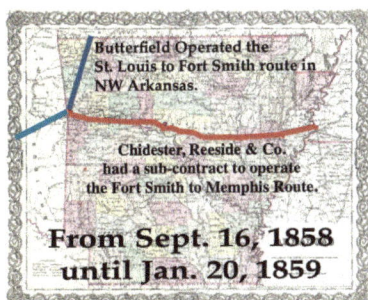
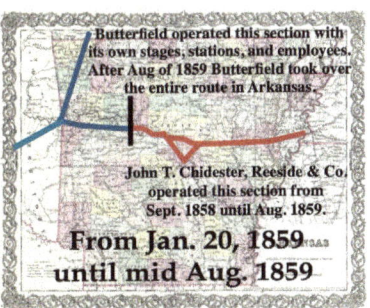

After August of 1859, giving up on the plan to use the steamboat Jennie Whipple between Fort Smith and Memphis, the Overland Mail Company ended their subcontract with Chidester, stocking the central Arkansas route with Butterfield owned stages, stations, horses and employees.

The Sale of Enslaved Workers and Rumors of Buried Treasure at Plummer's Station

"At the outbreak of the War between the States, Mr. Plummer realizing that the South's resources were limited compared to those of the North, and believing that all slaves would be freed, sold all of his slaves.

This act was to almost cost him his life at a later date.

*After General Lee's surrender, a band of **carpetbaggers** learned from local gossip that Mr. Plummer had sold his slaves for cash and had buried the money. They descended upon his home one night and demanded that he tell them where the money was hidden.*

He was living with his daughter at the time because his wife had died prior to the outbreak of the war. The carpetbaggers took him from the house to a large oak tree from which they proposed to hang him if he refused to reveal the hiding place of the money.

After long hours of questioning and threats, the raiders still received the same answer from Mr. Plummer--'I have no money buried.'

He must have convinced them, for they finally released him. However, rumor still persists that he did bury the money, and this is supported by the fact that no account was ever found of the money being used unless it was used to furnish leather supplies to the Southern troops during the war.

To this day, amateur treasure seekers often dig in the area surrounding the old Plummer home. If he did bury the money, he carried the secret to his grave."

The History of Plumerville, Arkansas by Elmer Mozingo

In the article above, the term 'carpetbaggers' refers to unscrupulous opportunists from the northern states who went to the South after the Civil War to profit from the Reconstruction.

Trail of Tears in Arkansas

Image compliments of the Northwest Arkansas Democrat & Gazette, March 25, 2014

The Trail of Tears & Plummer's Station

Plummer's home was visited by John Bell and Edward Deas during the removal of the Cherokee in December 1838, making it one of three remaining structures in Arkansas to bear witness to the Trail of Tears.

Historian Carolyn Yancy Kent writes, *"Samuel Plummer's place became a stopping place for travelers, and he became a supplier of rations for Indians being removed to Indian Territory and sold them corn, beef, and salt and fodder for the horses and livestock.*

In 1831, the first group of Indians, including Choctaw Peter Pitchlyn and eighteen or twenty Choctaw with 100 horses and nine enslaved persons, traveled on the road and arrived at Plummer's around December 20, 1831.

Between 1831 and 1838, many of the different Indian tribal groups traveling the road camped on his land. The Arkansas Gazette carried advertisements for the need for suppliers to give bids for rations for various tribes to be delivered to the groups at Plummer's, seven miles beyond the Cadron ferry. The last was a group of 660 Cherokee with John Adair Bell as conductor and Lieutenant Edward Deas as government agent; they were at Plummer's in December 1838. The mail carriers and then the mail and passenger stages began regular stops at Plummer's. A town was beginning to emerge. By 1859, he had given land for a campground to the Methodist Episcopal Church, South. When the railway was completed, stagecoach service stopped. In 1872, he sold a lot for a railroad station. He made one stipulation: no whiskey by the drink would be sold there.

On October 6, 1845, his wife died. Plummer died on February 15, 1876. Eleven children were born to the couple, but only three were alive in 1876. Of those three, only two were living in Plumerville, and the other was in California. Two of his sons died in the Civil War."
[Source: Carolyn Yancey Kent's paper, "Samuel Plummer (1800-1876)]."

Leaving Plummer's Station & Leather Shop, heading west, the next station stop for the Butterfield stagecoaches was at Lewisburg landing on the Arkansas River. Exactly, where was the station in Lewisburg?

Discovery of Markham Tavern
N 35.136316, W -92.736950

This is the story of a successful 4 year search to discover the location of Butterfield's swing station at Lewisburg, Arkansas.

My wife was born and grew up 1 mile from Lewisburg. I lived Morrilton for a short time in 1972. One would think we could discover the location of the Lewisburg station and the name of the station agent quickly. The search has taken four years instead.

A Little Background
Before We Begin our Search

In 1825 the town of Lewisburg was founded by Major William Lewis, along with his son Stephen Lewis and Dr. Nimrod Menefee. Sitting on the north side of the Arkansas River, Stephen D. Lewis established the first trading post in the county. In 1831 Lewisburg was named the county seat of Conway County, and a post office was established in 1832. Dr. Menefee donated the ground, and built a crude log house which served as the first court house for Conway County. This structure served as the courthouse during the Butterfield years, and was not replaced until 1873.

Lewisburg was incorporated in 1844, and was home to 80 businesses and 2,000 residents by 1850. This population supported two local newspapers, the *Wide-Awake*, and the *Western Empire*.

Before the railroad, Lewisburg was a lively river town and steamboat landing on the Arkansas River about midway between Little Rock and Fort Smith. Lewisburg served as the shipping and receiving port for all the produce for a large territory reaching north, almost to Missouri.

Steamboat Whipple, *drawn by David Garrison, Conte Crayon, 2010 a student at Southeastern Community College, West Burlington, Iowa*

John Butterfield's steamboat, Jennie Whipple, passed through or stopped at the port of Lewisburg Landing on only about 12 occasions when the Arkansas River water level was high enough for the trip. On the remaining 508 trips across Arkansas, Butterfield's stagecoaches stopped at Lewisburg for fresh horses.

Arrivals and Departures of the Jennie Whipple that included passing or stopping at the Lewisburg Landing

1858

Dec 22	departed Little Rock for Fort Smith
Dec __	arrived Fort Smith from Little Rock
Dec __	departed Fort Smith to Little Rock
Dec 28	arrived Little Rock from Fort Smith
Dec 29	departed Little Rock for Fort Smith

	1859
Jan __	arrived Fort Smith from Little Rock
Jan __	departed Fort Smith to Little Rock
Jan 3	arrived Little Rock from Fort Smith
Jan 4	departed Little Rock for Fort Smith
Jan __	arrived Fort Smith from Little Rock
Jan __	departed Fort Smith for Little Rock
Jan 8/9	arrived Little Rock from Fort Smith
Apr 9	departed Little Rock for Fort Smith
Apr __	arrived Fort Smith from Little Rock
Apr __	departed Fort Smith for Little Rock
Apr. 15	arrived Little Rock from Fort Smith
	1860
April __	departed Little Rock for Fort Smith

April 6 – "The Whipple still above Little Rock, with a heavy cargo for Fort Smith, awaiting a rise in order to get up."

May 8 – "Whipple is somewhere up in the Indian Nation, aground of course"

1861

Feb 20 – "...boats have been stuck there a year, Jennie Whipple being of them."

Feb __	departed Fort Smith for Little Rock
Feb __	arrived Little Rock from Fort Smith

[NOTE: At some point during this week in February, the Arkansas River level rose enough for her to steam downstream past Fort Smith to Little Rock. At Little Rock, she was held by the U.S. Marshal for payment of past due debts.]

Mar 9	departed Little Rock for Fort Smith
Apr 6	arrived Fort Smith from Memphis

[NOTE: This April 6th arrival at Fort Smith appears to be the last Overland Mail Co. trip across Arkansas. The last Overland mailbag left St. Louis on March 18, 1861 and arrived in Fort Smith about two days later, and in San Francisco April 13, 1861. Therefore this April 6th mailbag would have missed the last stage.]

Apr __	departed Fort Smith for Memphis
April 11	arrived Memphis from Fort Smith

On April 6, 1861 Butterfield sold the Jennie Whipple to a Mr. Adams for operation in the Dubuque, Iowa area of the Mississippi River. She was later used to transport Union troops and arms on the Mississippi during the Civil War. In 1866 the Jennie Whipple apparently sunk near the west end of Arkansas' White River cut off.

In the 1870's the railroad began to replace the steamboat as the preferred mode of travel in Arkansas.

The story is told that the Little Rock and Fort Smith Railroad offered to lay their tracks through Lewisburg, but the town refused to pay a $2,000 fee. As a result, the tracks were laid about 2 miles north of the town, and began scheduled service on November 21, 1870. Within 5 years residents of Lewisburg had begun to relocate north near the train depot, and the area near the depot was incorporated as a new town named "Morrilton."

History of Morrilton

Rachel Silva, employed by the Arkansas Historic Preservation Program, wrote a history of Morrilton in "Walks through History - Moose Addition Historic District" on June 14, 2014.

Brief History of Morrilton

" Conway County was established in 1825 by Arkansas's Territorial Legislature from part of Pulaski County and was named for Henry Wharton Conway, a member of the Arkansas Territory's delegation to the U.S. Congress. The county originally included present-day Conway, Faulkner, Van Buren, White, Cleburne, and Perry counties, along with part of Yell County.

In 1825 the town of Cadron, which was then located in the center of Conway County, became the temporary seat of government. As additional counties were carved out of the original Conway County, Conway County's seat of government moved around to whatever location was central and prosperous at the time. The county seat moved to Harrisburg in 1829 but was moved in 1831 to Lewisburg on the Arkansas River after Dr. Nimrod Menefee donated land for a courthouse and jail. In 1850 the county seat moved to Springfield, where it remained until 1873, when it returned to Lewisburg.

Lewisburg was established as a trading post in 1825 by early settlers Major William Lewis and his son, Stephen D. Lewis, and was located on the Arkansas River about one mile southeast of present-day Morrilton. In 1844 Lewisburg incorporated as a town and had a population of about 2,000.

The community thrived due to its location on the Arkansas River, which was the best transportation route for people and products at that time. In the 1850s, Lewisburg boasted over 80 businesses, including two sawmills, two gristmills, a flour mill, cotton gin, hotels, saloons, and numerous stores. However, the arrival of the railroad would change everything.

In the 1850s, the Little Rock and Fort Smith Railroad surveyed a route through land near Lewisburg, but construction was interrupted by the Civil War. When construction resumed after the war, the railroad company asked the residents of Lewisburg for a financial contribution to help defray costs. Lewisburg declined to provide the money for two reasons—residents were financially devastated after the Civil War, and they thought that the town's strategic position would necessitate its inclusion along the route. Well, they were wrong, and the LR & Fort Smith Railroad bypassed Lewisburg, building its tracks about one mile north of the river town through land donated by Edward Henry Morrill and James Miles Moose.

The railroad reached present-day Morrilton in 1871, and the first depot was a boxcar called "Lewisburg Station," although it was located more than a mile from the town. The first bona fide railroad station was established in 1873 on land given by E. H. Morrill, and the first station agent, Captain J. W. Boot is credited with naming the town, choosing between Morrill and Moose by the flip of a coin.

Morrilton was first spelled with two 'L's, like its namesake. The population slowly moved from Lewisburg to Morrilton, and the new town incorporated in 1880 with a population of about 800. In 1883 Morrilton became the Conway County seat and remains so today.

...After the Civil War, Mr. Moose moved the 1835 Markham Tavern building from Lewisburg to 711 Green Street and added to it to make his residence..."

This 'History of Morrilton' answered many questions except one: - Where did the stagecoaches of Butterfield stop 508 times in Lewisburg for fresh horses between September 1858 and March 1861?

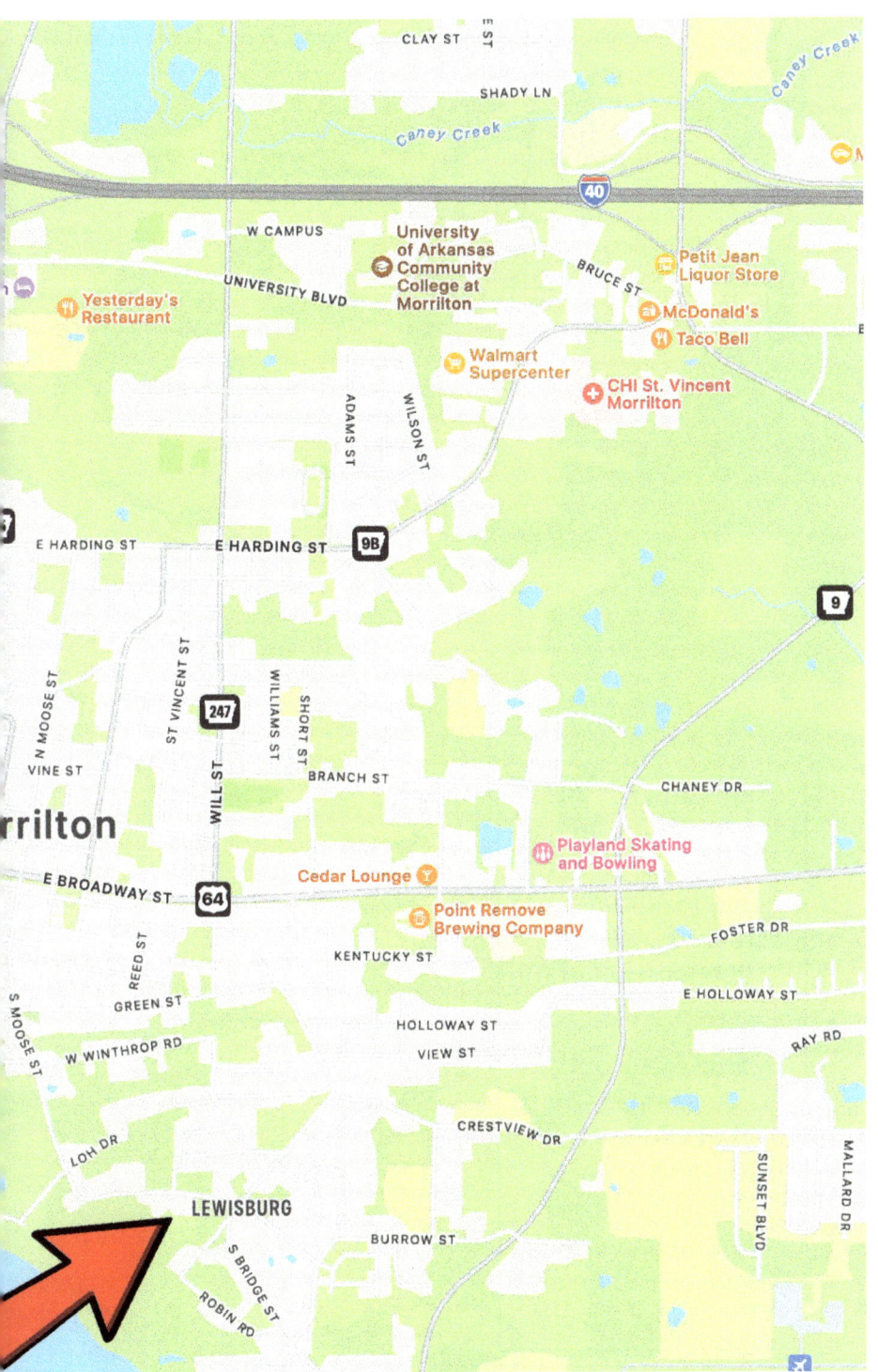

Butterfield Overland National Historic Trail Through Arkansas' Pope & Conway Counties

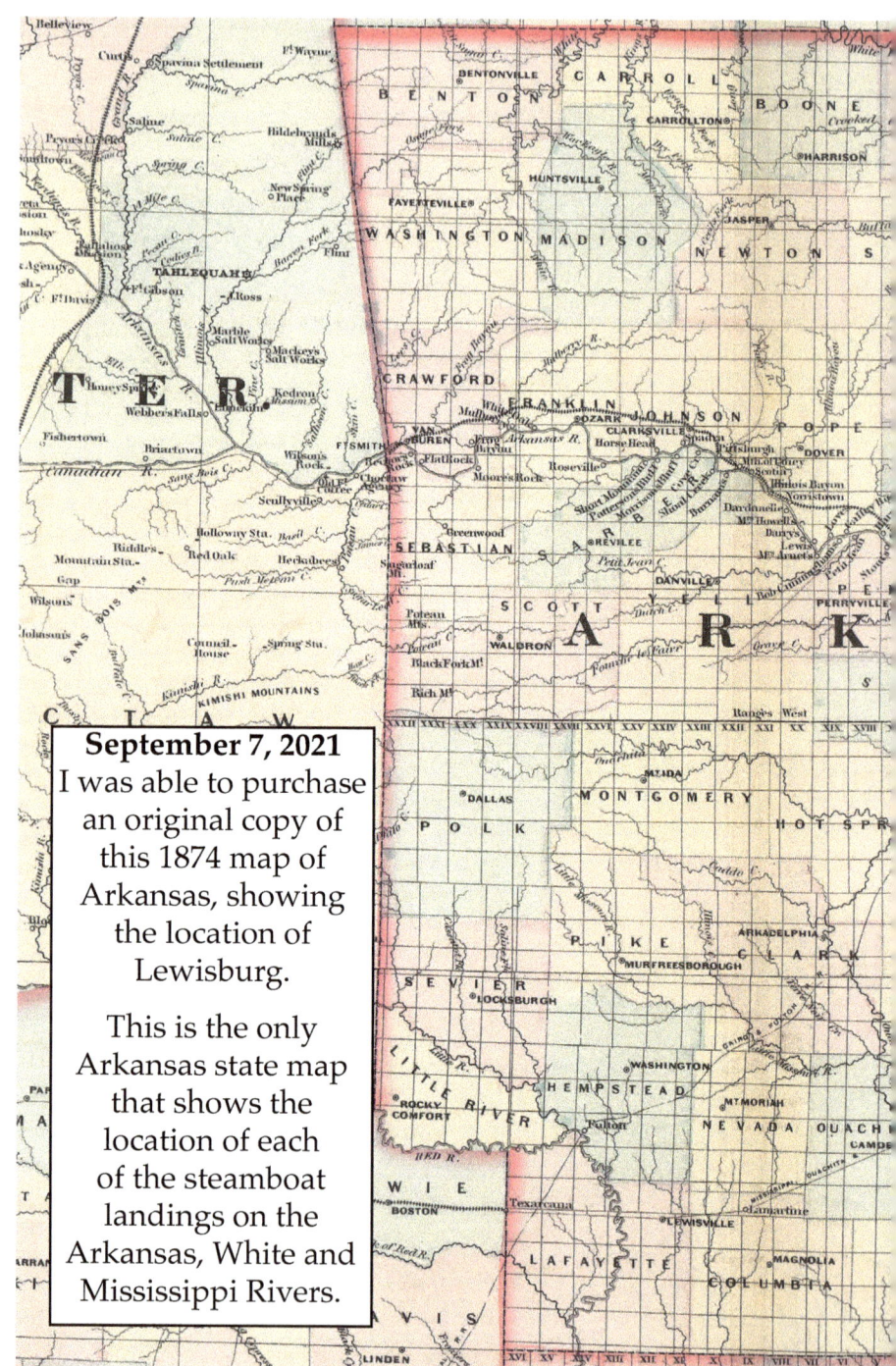

September 7, 2021
I was able to purchase an original copy of this 1874 map of Arkansas, showing the location of Lewisburg.

This is the only Arkansas state map that shows the location of each of the steamboat landings on the Arkansas, White and Mississippi Rivers.

Butterfield Overland National Historic Trail Through Arkansas' Pope & Conway Counties

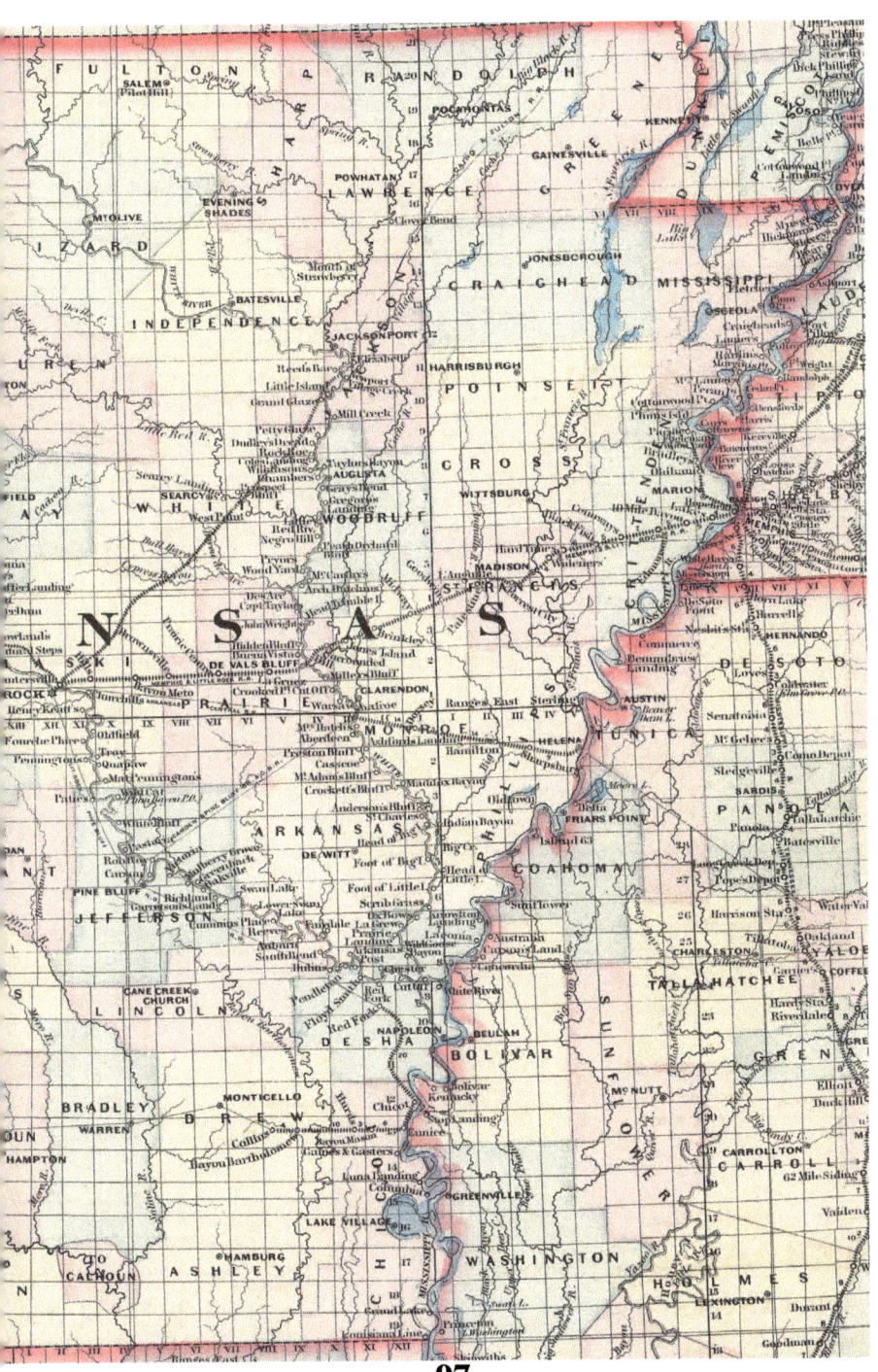

This cropped section of the 1874 state map, shows the relationship of Lewisburg to Little Rock and the other steamboat landings along the Arkansas River. This particular map does not show the 1827 Old Mil-

Butterfield Overland National Historic Trail Through Arkansas' Pope & Conway Counties

itary Road used by Butterfield, but it does show the proposed route for the railroad that closely paralleled the BUTTERFIELD OVERLAND NATIONAL HISTORIC TRAIL

*1874 Asher & Adams Arkansas and portion of Indian Territory
Original map from the collection of Bob Crossman*

The Search Begins

Between 2020 and 2024, I made several trips to the Conway County History Museum located in the old railroad depot in downtown Morrilton, Arkansas.

"City of Lewisburg 1852" by Susan Gordon Stout
Courtesy of the Conway County History Museum in the railroad depot

The Conway County History Museum has on display a wonderful painting of Lewisburg as it appeared in 1852. The museum volunteers did not know the name or location of any stage stop or livery stable Butterfield may have used in Lewisburg.

This painting is shown shortly after its discovery, before it was professionally cleaned and restored.

There is a great story behind this painting. A May 10, 2007 article in the *Arkansas Gazette* reports that Jackie Guccione of Russellville, Arkansas had great grandparents who lived in Lewisburg. In May of 2006, while helping her sister in Batesville, Jackie came across an oil painting. Initially her sister put a $5 price on the painting and placed it on a table during her garage sale.

When the painting didn't sell, Jackie took the painting home and began to do some research. In a history of Conway County she found a black and white reproduction of the painting in question. Checking back with her sister in Batesville, she discovered the painting had been given to her by a relative of the original artist.

Jackie Guccione and Conway County genealogist Euna Beavers pieced together the story of the painting's origin. They determined that the painting was the work of Susan Gordon, a young woman in a prominent Lewisburg family.

Gucciune believes the painting was completed around 1870, when the artist was 20 years old. The painting depicts Lewisburg circa 1852. Gucciune speculated that the artist was trying to capture the best days of Lewisburg to generate hope during the difficult Reconstruction days following the Civil War. "My best speculation was that (Susan Gordon) painted it while she was pregnant with her child. After the Civil War, Reconstruction was a tough time in Lewisburg and Conway County. I think she was trying to paint a painting showing how peaceful life was there before the war."

A few years after completing the painting, the artist Susan Gordon died because of complications during childbirth. Several years later, her family moved away from Lewisburg.

In the same article *("Door to the Past: History of Lewisburg to Be Celebrated Saturday,"* May 7, 2007, *Arkansas Democrat Gazette* by Jeff LeMaster), Euna Beavers said, *"A remnant of the old Gordon home was recently found in what used to be Lewisburg, which is just south of modern-day Morrilton."* Beavers and several others set out looking for artifacts from the area and found more than expected.

Euna Beavers reported, *"We found the rock footer of the Gordon's house. We knew it was their house because there were two magnolia trees in what would have been their front yard. In everything we've read and even in Miss Gordon's painting, those two trees are there. We found three or four foundations and a few wells and cisterns. It's private property and it's grown up and very heavily wooded.*

After the Civil War, *"a lot of the buildings were gone. A lot of them were in really bad shape. Some of the ones that were still good, the people tore down and took the materials to build their homes in Morrilton.*

One thing depicted in Gordon's painting is **the Markham Tavern..."**

The old Markham Tavern

Cropped from copy of Susan Gordan's original by D. Imhauser, 2008

**The Morrilton Depot Museum
is now called Conway County History Museum**

Morrilton's Conway County History Museum is located in the old railroad depot at 101 East Railroad Avenue. The museum is open, free of charge, Friday and Saturday from 10:00 am to 2:00 pm. These three photographs of old Lewisburg are on display.

Lewisburg Ferry, *ca. 1900*
Image courtesy of Conway County History Museum in Morrilton's Depot

Lewisburg Ferry, *ca. 1917*
*Will Hardin (left) and Frank Robinson, who was the father-in-law of Charles Isely
Image courtesy of Conway County History Museum in Morrilton's Depot*

Road to Morrilton from Lewisburg Ferry, *by Thos. H. Jerome, ca. 1900*
*The Lewisburg community, with several hundred residents, is now on the south side of today's Morrilton. Only one or two of the homes look like they might have existed in 1858-1861. In the 1870's many of the Lewisburg residents disassembled their houses to relocate them one mile north to be near the new railroad depot in Morrilton.
Image courtesy of Conway County History Museum in Morrilton's Depot*

Morrilton's Conway County History Museum also has on display, in the railroad depot, this photo of the Arkansas River ferry crossing site as seen from Lewisburg.

The Arkansas River at Lewisburg ca. 1900
Image courtesy of the Conway County History Museum

Ferry Site at Lewisburg

"The first ferry at Lewisburg was run by a Mr. McKnabb, and was established about 1848... Mr. McKnabb was followed by John Willis, then Grary & Hines, who sold to Thomas S. Haynes. In 1866, it fell into the possession of A. C. Wells... In 1888 it was bought by R. D. Morgan, who built a strong and suitable boat - side wheel boat, 63 feet in length and 18 feet beam... Early in 1890 it was purchased with the ferry privilege by W. P. Wells and John Ward, by whom it is conducted now (1890)." [Historical Reminisces of Conway County, 1890, page 35]

The Lewisburg Ferry was used until 1920, when the bridge across the Arkansas River was built.

Concerning operators of the Lewisburg ferry, *"Horace Farish, Frank Robinson, and Ed Hurdin were the operators until Charles Isley and his partner Charlie McArthur bought it from the widow of Dr. White. Mr. Isley operated it until the old river bridge was opened."* [Conway County - Our Land, Our Home, Our People, Second Edition, page 13]

The Arkansas At Lewisburg

December 24, 2020

On December 24, 2020, my wife and I made our first trip to find a cemetery in Lewisburg. We discovered that there are two - the "Lewisburg Cemetery" and the "Old Lewisburg Cemetery" that overlooks the Arkansas River.

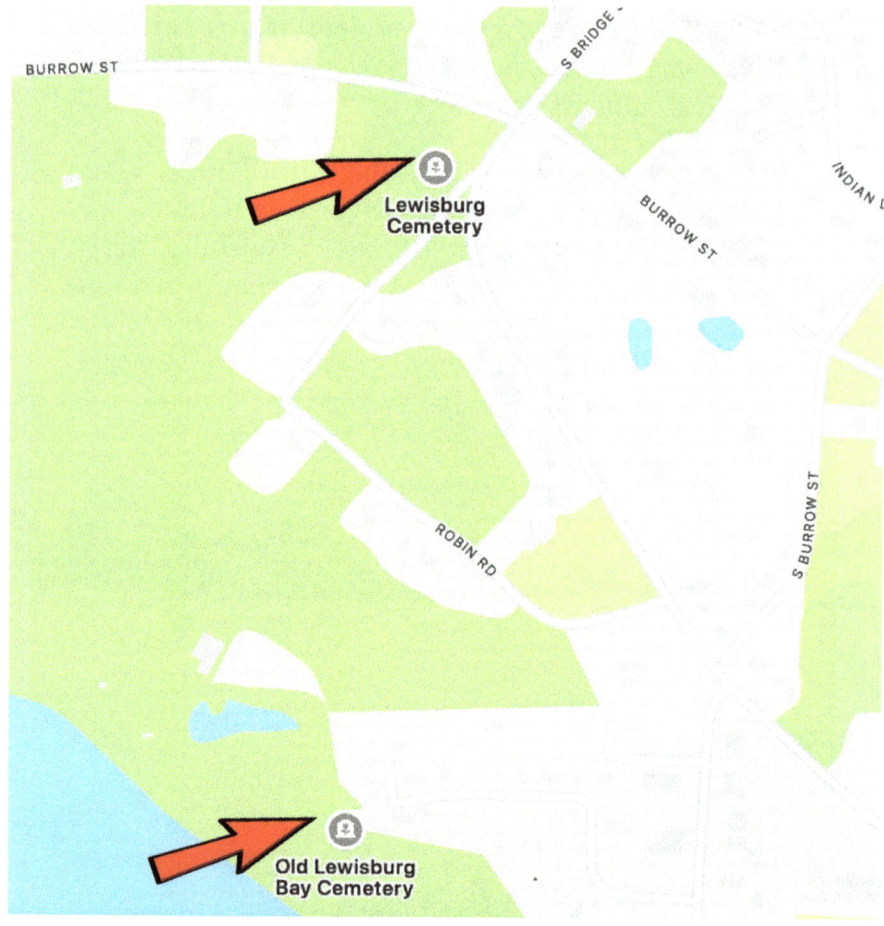

In the Lewisburg Cemetery we found 102 graves dating from John Ewing McClure (1790-1835) to the most recent, Carl E. Dickson (1938-2018).

In the Lewisburg Cemetery we found the grave of my wife's great aunt, Maggie Hamlet Cureton. (Dec. 20, 1890 - Jan 26, 1930) (shown at right)

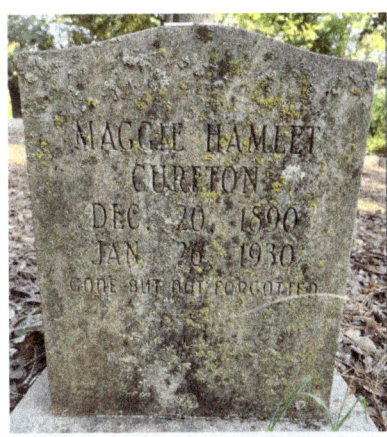

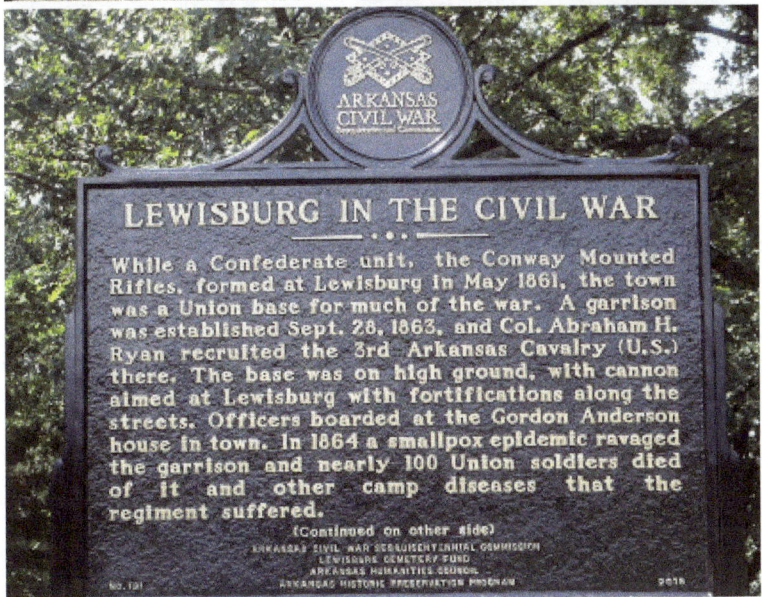

A few months later, on the south side of Lewisburg, we found the Old Lewisburg Cemetery. It contains 37 graves dating from Harriet B. Lewis Menefee (1803-1828) to the most recent, Sarah M Krueger Weckwerth (1897 - 1996). The Old Lewisburg cemetery overlooks the Arkansas River. *Photos below by Bob Crossman*

Discovering Newspaper Articles About Lewisburg
January 2021

In January of 2021, historic newspapers of Arkansas were searched in hopes of finding a mention of the stage stop or a livery stable at Lewisburg.

The search was not successful.

However, an advertisement by "N. Menefee & Co." was found in the Aug. 25, 1832 newspapers, four years before the Arkansas Territory gained statehood:

Lots for Sale In the Town of Lewisburg

A second sale of lots in this town will be offered for sale at the next September term of the County Court, commencing on Monday the 17th day of said month, on credit of six and twelve months, purchasers giving bond and approved security.

Lewisburg is beautifully situated on the north bank of the Arkansas river, 45 or 50 miles above Little Rock, and it is believed; unites more advantages in point of locality of situation and fertility of the adjacent country, than any town in the Territory. It is situated between the two flourishing settlements of Peconery below, and Point Remove above, and a most excellent body of land on the opposite side of the river, including Esq'r Ellis settlement, and extending southwest as far as the prosperous settlement of Forche-la-Favre. Northeast from Lewisburg, for 8 or 10 miles, the country is gently rolling interspersed with a few rich prairies, until you reach the rich bottoms of cane and cypress, and the north fork of Cadron and sources of Point Remove; all of which are very fertile and susceptible of extensive settlements. — Further on in the same direction, you strike the very flourishing settlement (the most remote in the country) of Little Red river, known by the name of Rich Woods, or New Kentucky. This picturesque healthy and fertile section of the country is settling rapidly with an enterprising, industrious class of citizens...

Within a few hundred yards to the town is a fine bold

never-failing chalybeate spring, and also a spring of pure water — building materials of every description are in great abundance on and near the premises, such as clay suitable for brick, an excellent stone quarry, and extensive groves of fine timber...

An article was found in the Dec. 9, 1840 issue of the *Arkansas Gazette* describing one of the worst disasters of early steamboating in Arkansas: *"On Thursday last about 10 o'clock a.m. the steamboat* CHEROKEE, *C. Harris, master, bound for Fort Gibson, stopped at Lewisburg, about 15 miles above this city, to land passengers. She had not been at the landing more than 10 minutes before her boilers exploded, sweeping right and left, from midship forward, every part from the guards up. One boiler was thrown into the river, the other on shore, making the most dreadful havoc of human life than can be imagined. One man was thrown up in the air 200 feet and fell in the town some distance from the river bank; 17 other persons were killed, their blackened corpses mangled in the most shocking manner. From nine to fourteen persons known to have been on board are missing; 18 or 20 persons are severely injured, some burned, some scalded, others with broken legs, heads and arms, presenting, as we are informed by an eye witness, a scene too horrid for description."* [Arkansas Gazette, Dec. 9, 1840]

Also, an article was found in the June 30, 1976 *Petit Jean County Headlight* depicting a photograph of E. H. Morrill. A coin toss between James Moose and E. H. Morrill had decided the town's name: 'Morrilton.'

Although this search through old newspapers did not reveal the location of the Butterfield station, Lewisburg did make the newspapers on a different subject. One of Butterfield's employees, George Crull, was accused of arson and abolitionist activities.

This story ran in multiple newspapers between April 14, 1860 and April 22, 1860. They are reproduced below.

April 14, 1860
Overland Driver, George Crull, Accused of Arson & Abolitionist Activities

April 14, 1860
Arkansas True Democrat, Little Rock, Arkansas
FIRE IN LEWISBURG, ARKANSAS, APRIL 9, 1860 –
MESSRS. JOHNSON & YERKES –
GENTS: I hasten to drop you a few lines of my own and other's misfortune: on yesterday morning (Sunday) about 8 o'clock by the gin house in this town, containing some 50 or 60 bales of cotton was discovered to be on fire. As soon as the alarm was given, the citizens and some of the neighbors responded very promptly, and rendered active and valuable service.

Soon afterwards the gin house of M. T. T. Henry, successor to Henry & Co., of this place, containing some 15 bales of cotton, was discovered to be on fire. Between these gins stood my large warehouse, which contained a large amount of cotton, beef hides, poultry and firs, together with a large amount of groceries and other goods – very soon it took fire from my gin, when all three of the buildings with nearly all of their contents were destroyed.

The work was undoubtedly from an incendiary; and I think one **George Crull, an Overland Stage Driver** did it, or knew who did – *we drove him off.* It seems that the fire was by a slow match to each of the lint rooms of the gins, as they were both found to be on fire *near the same time.* By hard work we prevented the fire from extending to any other house.

Article about racial tension with Butterfield employees.

My individual loss will be about		$5,000.00
Myself and R. B. Griffin	"	5,000.00
Dr. F. W. Adams	"	2,500.00
T. T. Henry	"	1,200.00
R. Welborn	"	300.00
T. W. Barber	"	500.00
Jno. Breedon	"	300.00
R. Simpson	"	150.00
N. S. Williams	"	100.00
Sundry other persons	"	<u>250.00</u>
Total loss		$15,300.00

There was no insurance on any of the loss unless it was on Mr. T. W. Barber's which was in transportation. There was some 10 or 12 hundred dollars worth of cotton and other goods saved for various persons in a damaged condition. The citizens and friends – one and all – will please accept my most heartfelt thanks for their very extraordinary efforts to save the property. – *Your Friend, Anderson Gordon*

[NOTE: The article above was also printed in the April 14, 1860, issue of the *Arkansas Banner*.]

April 21, 1860
OVERLAND DRIVERS ACCUSED OF: ENCOURAGING SLAVES TO REVOLT, ATTEMPTING TO STEAL SLAVES, AND AFTER A MOB WHIPPED A BUTTERFIELD DRIVER SETTING A FIRE TO SEVERAL BUILDINGS NEAR THE LEWISBURG BUTTERFIELD STATION

April 21, 1860, Saturday, page 3
Arkansas Banner, Little Rock Arkansas
ABOLITION EMISSARIES AMONGST US – DESTRUCTIVE FIRE

Lewisburg, Ark., April 13, 1860 – MR. EDITOR: I write this for the purpose of putting our people, if possible, on the alert – it really seems as if a lethargy had seized them that could not be thrown off.

On Saturday the 7th of April, the Democrats held a

township meeting in Lewisburg, and then we learned for the first time the concerted operations of the **Overland Mail Stage Employees** in our midst.

They had persuaded Dr. Menefee's negros to revolt, and the project was nearly ripe for execution, when the affair was divulged to him by a trusty old negro woman.

One of the *[Butterfield]* drivers acknowledged the facts as related to Menefee by the negro; and the Doctor, I suppose, in his anger and surprise forgot that the statute of our State *[of Arkansas]* would have *dealt* with him very severely. He told him *[the Butterfield driver]* to leave and he did so.

A citizen of our town overheard one of these men *[Butterfield drivers]* tell a negro that if he would wait until he made money enough stage driving, he would take him off *[help him escape slavery]* where a negro is a good as a white man. *[Perhaps referring to New York, the home of many of the Butterfield employees.]*

He *[Butterfield driver George Crull]* was whipped and told to leave, and he did not wait for a second warning.

So, hearing that there were two others left of the same sort *[apparently referring to two additional Butterfield employees - perhaps from the Butterfield swing station there in Lewisburg]* a committee of citizens was appointed to wait on them and ascertain the facts. We were not disposed to punish innocent men, and having nothing tangible to operate on, we merely read them the *"riot act."*

In consequence of these proceedings, these men *[Butterfield drivers]* either in person or by proxy fired by slow matches the gin houses of A. Gordon and T. T. Henry, esq., which also consumed the warehouse of the first named gentlemen, situated between the

Article about racial tension with Butterfield employees.

Article about racial tension with Butterfield employees.

two gins. The loss to these gentlemen is very large, besides many others; back country merchants who had large freights stored in the warehouse. Estimated loss $20,000, and no insurance. We have heard of several other buildings being tried around the neighborhood; but believe the damage was inconsiderable compared with the above. *[NOTE: Apparently the **Butterfield** employees are also accused of unsuccessfully attempting to set fire to additional buildings.]*

These men *[**Butterfield** employees]* are still running at large and the public should use caution against all suspicious characters lurking in their midst.

We have determined if we cannot get our mail matter without having it brought by gin burners and negro stealers that we will dispense with it entirely.

signed, Vigilance

[NOTE: The letter to the Editor reproduced above is also printed in the Arkansas True Democrat, in the April 21, 1860 issue on page 3.]

At the time, the public whipping of a **Butterfield driver** George Crull, echoed national tensions. This 1856 image depicts U.S. Senator Charles Sumner being beaten thirty times by Congressmen Preston Brooks in the Senate chambers. Sumner, of Massachusetts was accused of being an anti-slavery abolitionists by Congressman Preston Brooks from South Carolina.

April 21, 1860
Lewisburg Slavery Story Continues
John Butterfield Asked to Only Hire "Southern Men"

April 21, 1860, Saturday, page 3
Arkansas True Democrat, Little Rock Arkansas

From Conway County – Lewisburg, Conway County, Arkansas – Mr. Editor – The citizens of this county held a meeting in Lewisburg, on Saturday April 7, and passed the following resolution:

Whereas, there has been an effort made in this county by certain transient persons *[Butterfield drivers]*, whom we have good reason to believe are abolition emissaries, to interfere with our slaves, and persuade them to assume an attitude of hostility to their masters; and whereas, we are determined to take action against all such, both vigorous and effective.

Resolved, That we hereby advise all suspicious men having no employment amongst us, and who are drifting about for the purpose of injuring us in the possession of our property *[slaves]*, to cease from this day any intermeddling in our domestic institutions, else we pledge them and ourselves, that we will deal with them *[more whippings]* with the utmost rigor.

Resolved, That the chair appoint a committee of seven to wait on the agents of the **Overland** and Fort Smith and Little Rock mail lines, and request the removal of all employees, except such as are known to be good southern men, and to engage no others. *[**Butterfield** should only hire southern men who support slavery.]*

Resolved, That the persons subscribing hereto shall constitute a vigilance committee, any five of whom shall have power to carry out these resolutions in spirit and effect. *[The forty signers of this resolution will serve as a vigilante mob to whip and run off any anti-slavery men.]*

Article about racial tension with Butterfield employees.

RESOLVED, That the Little Rock papers be requested to publish these proceedings.

The chair appointed as the committee Messrs. S. H. Nieman, R. Welborn, L. O. Breeden, A. Gordon, R. T. Markham, W. L. Menefee and R. W. Harper.

S. J. Stallings, Chairman
and forty others.

The racial tensions in these newspaper articles are reflected on the back side of the historical marker at the Lewisburg Cemetery.

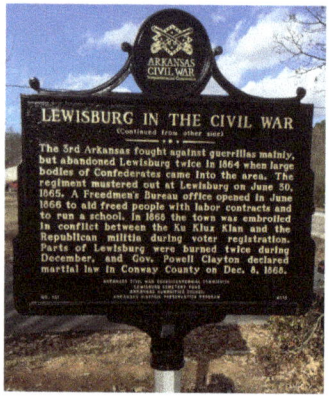

Historical Marker at the Lewisburg Cemetery
1099 Mockingbird Lane, Morrilton, AR

"*A Freedmen's Bureau office opened in June 1866 to aid freed people with labor contracts and to run a school. In 1868 the town was embroiled in conflict between the Ku Klux Klan and the Republican Militia during voter registration. Parts of Lewisburg were burned twice during December, and Gov. Powell Clayton declared Martial Law in Conway County on Dec. 8, 1868.*"

The National Park Service web site article, "Fort Smith's United States Colored Troops" states: *"The 11th Regiment, United States Colored Troops was recruited out of Fort Smith in the fall of 1863, shortly after the Union had recaptured the post from Confederate forces... [Nov. 1864] they left western Arkansas for Lewisburg, a town near Little Rock. Five months later...*

January 7, 2021

On January 7, 2021, in an effort to discover the Butterfield stage station in Lewisburg, a visit was made to the public library in nearby Morrilton, Arkansas.

The library is located at 101 West Church Street in the county seat, Morrilton, Arkansas. The Classical Revival style building was designed by Thomas Harding and funded in part by a grant from Andrew Carnegie.

Morrilton Mayor J. A. Frisby, Night Rainwater, and W. M. Riddick gave the land for the library.

With a $10,000 grant, the construction cost was $7,500, and the furniture and a supply of heating coal cost $2,500. Construction was completed in October of 1916 and still serves as the Conway County Library today. In 1978 the building was listed on the National Register of Historic Places. This library began in various Morrilton homes as a private book collection in 1894, and was moved to the new building in 1916.

A map was discovered on this visit (see next page).

Morrilton Public Library, 1916

Butterfield Overland National Historic Trail Through Arkansas' Pope & Conway Counties

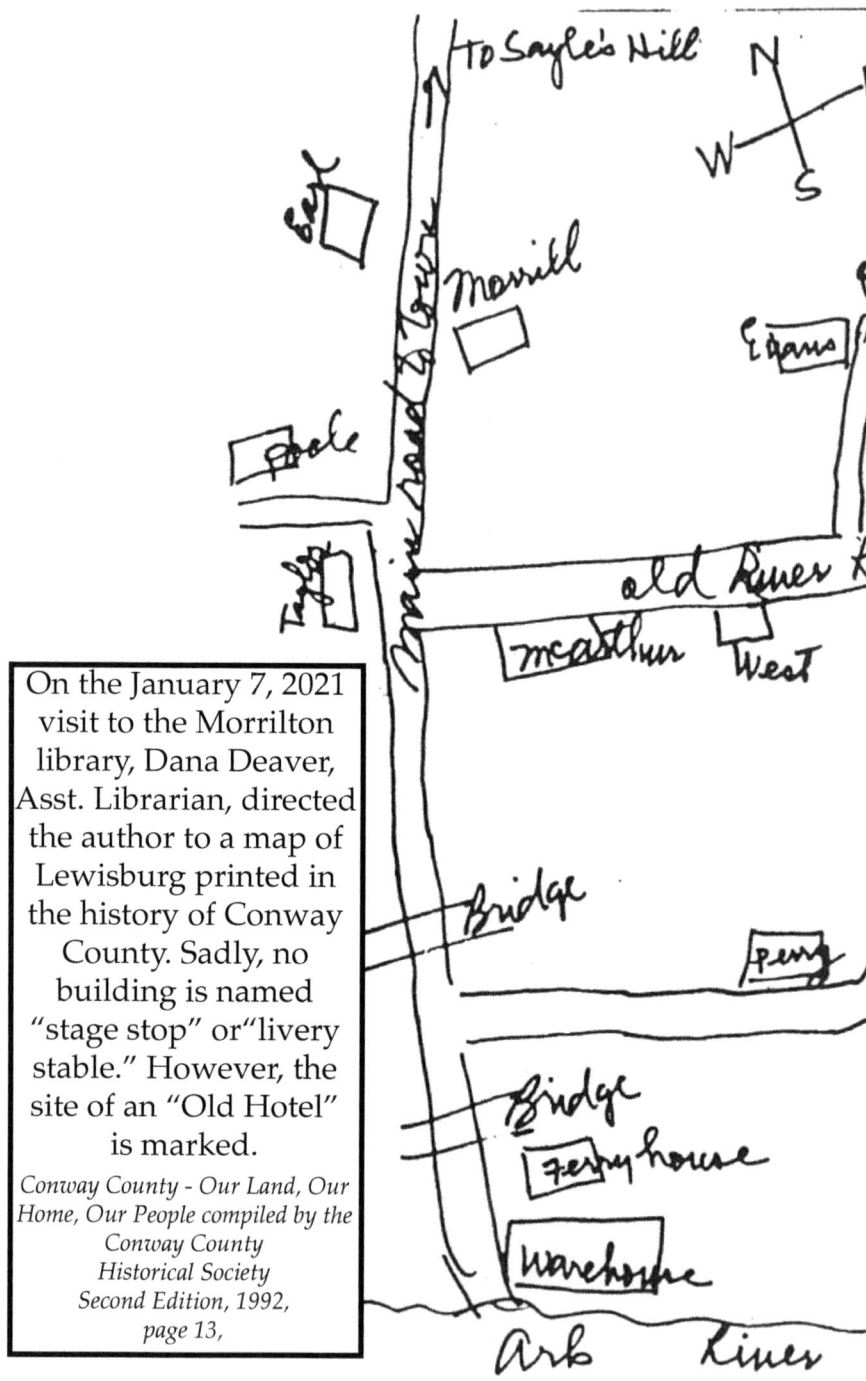

On the January 7, 2021 visit to the Morrilton library, Dana Deaver, Asst. Librarian, directed the author to a map of Lewisburg printed in the history of Conway County. Sadly, no building is named "stage stop" or "livery stable." However, the site of an "Old Hotel" is marked.

Conway County - Our Land, Our Home, Our People compiled by the Conway County Historical Society Second Edition, 1992, page 13.

© 2024 Robert O. Crossman

Butterfield Overland National Historic Trail Through Arkansas' Pope & Conway Counties

Old Lewisburg

© 2024 Robert O. Crossman

August 25, 2023

On August 25, 2023 the author discovered a map that displays the street layout of old Lewisburg.

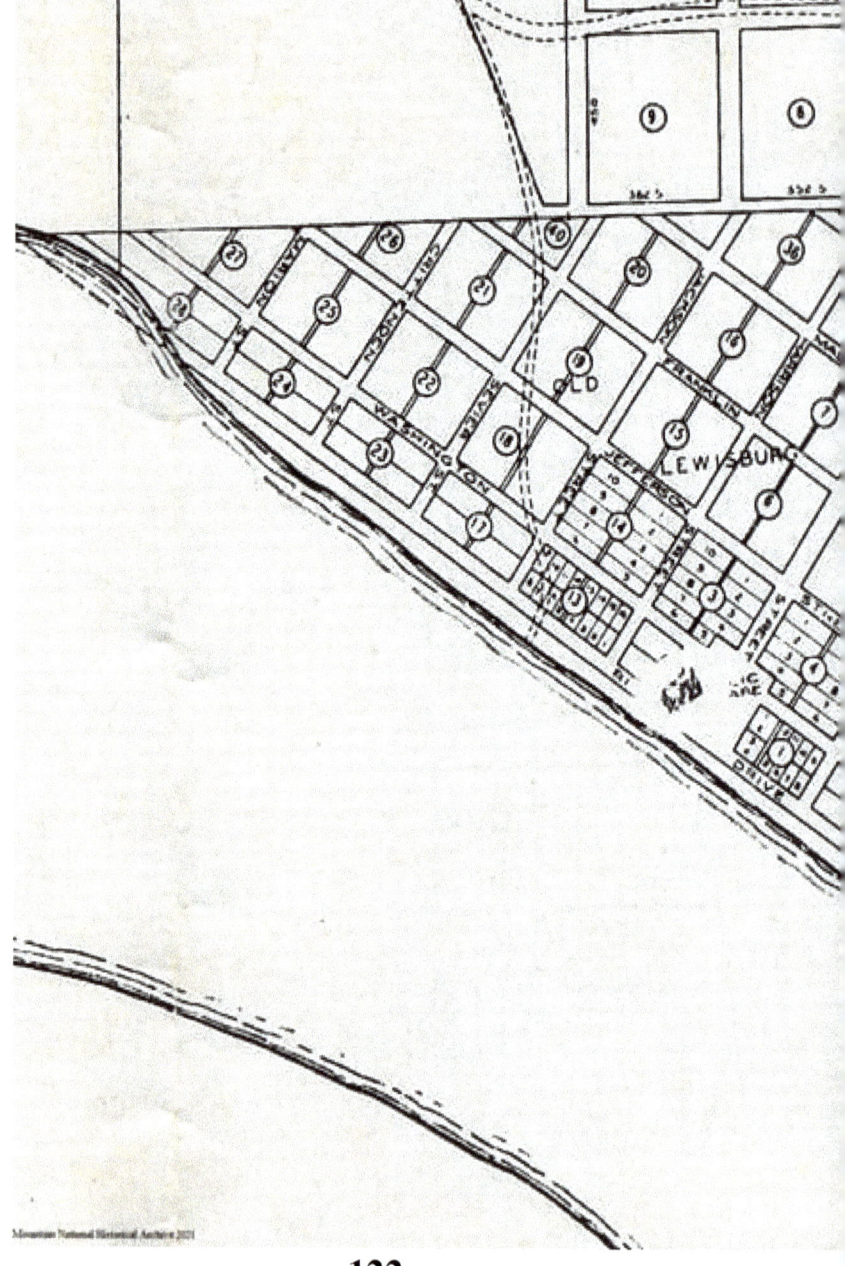

Sadly, there is no indication of a stage stop or livery stable's location on this street layout.
The current streets are indicated with dotted lines.

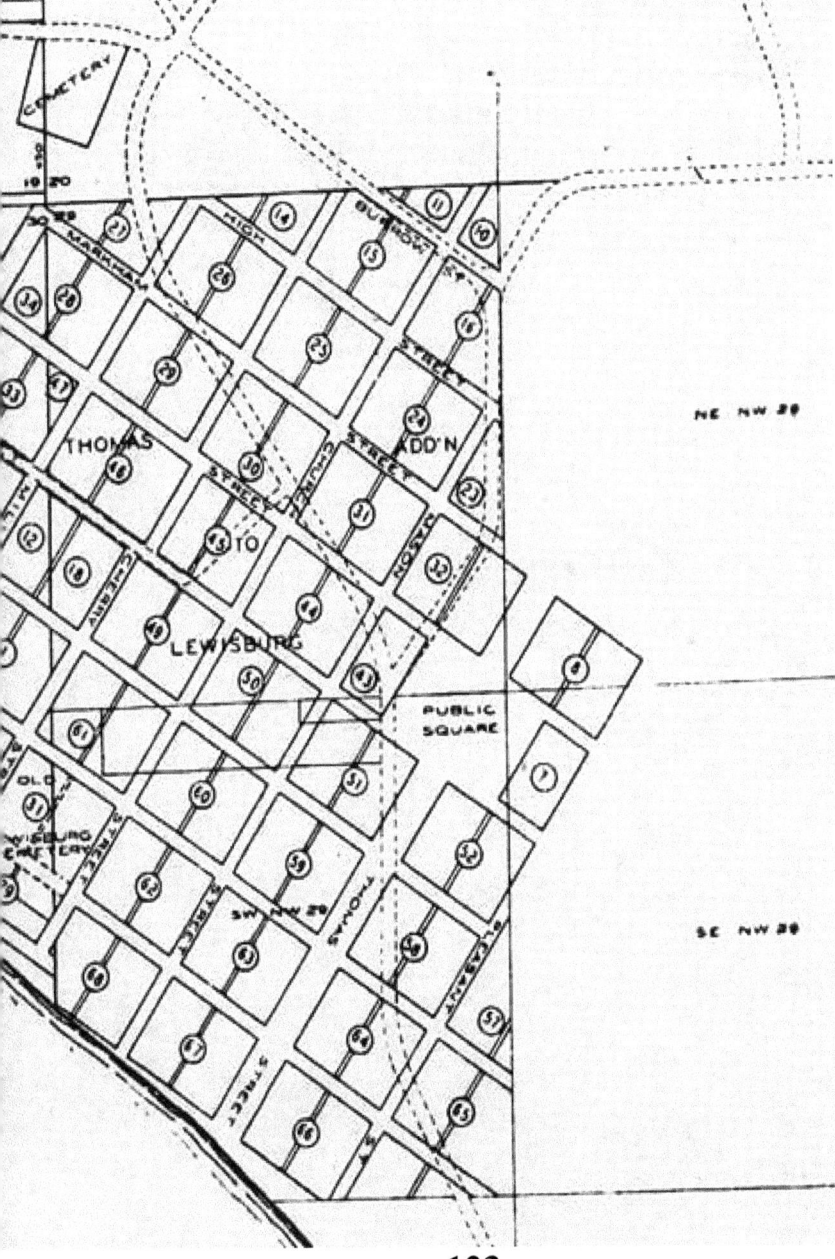

Butterfield Overland National Historic Trail Through Arkansas' Pope & Conway Counties

November 2023

In November of 2023, contact was made with the Arkansas State Surveyor, Daniel Phillips, seeking to locate the precise route of the 1828 Old Military Road through Lewisburg

In December of 2023 he provided a survey map from the 1850's. This wonderful survey shows the 1827 Old Military Road that connected Little Rock and Fort Smith.

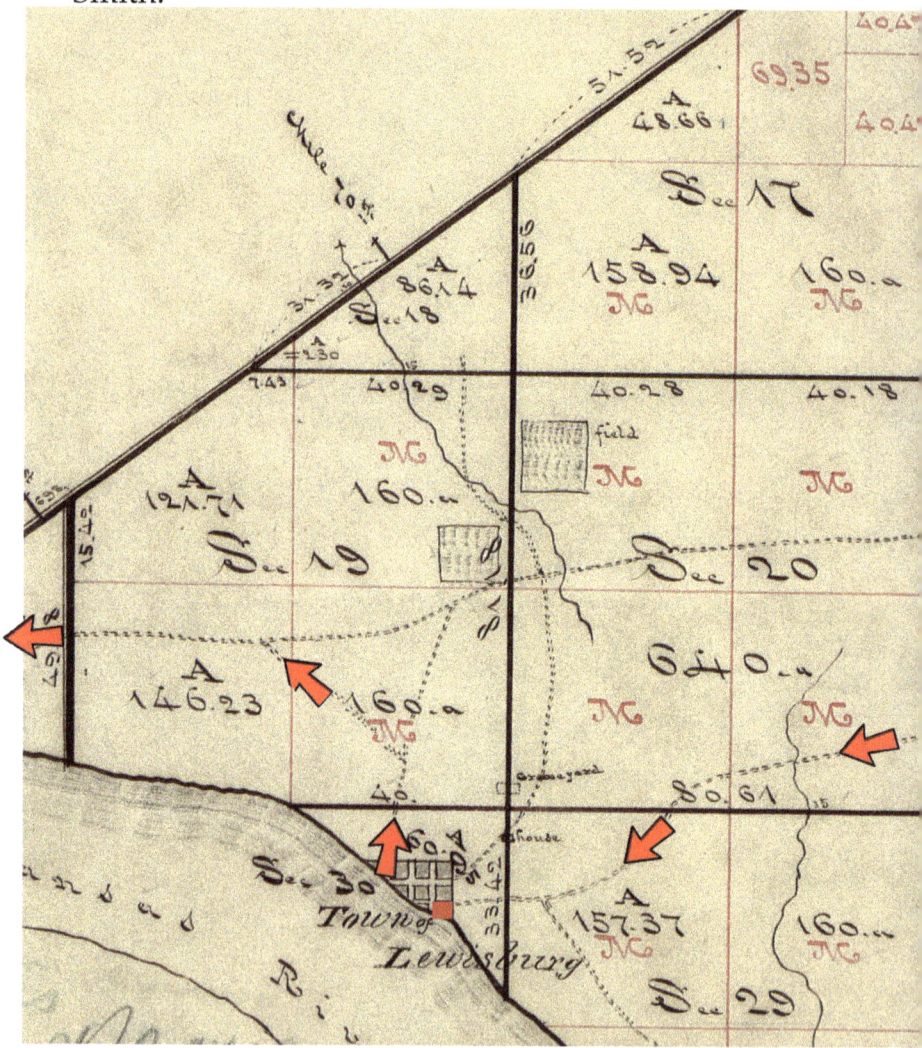

The Military Road passes just north of the town of Lewisburg, so a "stage road" branched off of the Old Military Road to connect the town to this major east-west Military Road.

The author has added arrows to highlight the route followed by the stagecoaches along the Butterfield Overland National Historic Trail.

April 1, 2024

The 1st Solid Clue

On April 1, 2024, I posted on the "Remember Morrilton" Facebook page, asking if anyone could help *"find the name of the stage stop owner or livery stable in Lewisburg."*

Janice McConnell Malone replied, suggesting that I search the US Census. Following up on her suggestion, the 1860 census for Lewisburg Township, Conway County, Arkansas offered several clues.

Below is a list of the Lewisburg residents the 1860 census with stagecoach related occupations:

Reuben T. Markham, 35 year old "Hotel Keeper" born in Alabama.

Berrilla T. Markham, 25 year old "Asst. House" born in Tennessee.

A hostler and two stage drivers were staying at the Markham Hotel at the time of the census:

Benj Cartright, an 18 year old male hostler born in Mississippi.(*A hostler was "employed to look after the horses in a stable or at an Inn'*)

Chas Lowe, a 25 year old male stage driver

E. Wallington, a 24 year old stage driver born in Vermont.

Others in the Lewisburg Township 1860 Census with stagecoach related occupations, include:

Samuel T. Collins, a 31 year old male blacksmith born in Virginia;

Lemuel Autry, a 48 year old blacksmith born in South Carolina;

Paul M. Autry, a 25 year old apprentice blacksmith born in Mississippi;

H. Hathaway, a 35 year old teamster born in Maine;

Jno F. Porter, a 41 year old male, saddler born in Kentucky; and

Jno B. H. Tyler, a 33 year old blacksmith born in Kentucky.

Based on these census occupations, it may very well be that the Lewisburg Butterfield Stage stop was at Rueben T. Markham's Tavern. This brought us one step toward confirming that Markham Tavern was the swing station for Butterfield's Overland Mail Company stagecoaches.

Arkansas Hotels were often used by Butterfield as stage stops such as the Anthony Hotel in Little Rock, the Jackson Hotel in Des Arc, the Atlanta Hotel in Oakland Grove and also the City Hotel and St. Charles Hotel in Fort Smith, Arkansas.

At this point I did not have a definitive answer for the location of the Butterfield stagecoach stop in Lewisburg - but this was the best lead we've had so far.

April 2, 2024
The 2nd Solid Clue, and Family Confirmation

Digging deeper to discover Butterfield's Lewisburg stage station, I discovered a 2007 interview of the great granddaughter of Reuben T. Markham.

In May 7, 2007, Jeff LeMaster wrote an article for the Arkansas Democrat Gazette, *"Door to the Past: History of Lewisburg to Be Celebrated Saturday."* In the article he reports on an interview with Jackie Guccione and Euna Beavers.

Jackie is great granddaughter of Markham Tavern owner, Ruben T. Markham. Jackie told the reporter, that **Markham Tavern was** a rest stop for river travelers and **A STAGECOACH RELAY STATION ON THE BUTTERFIELD TRAIL BETWEEN MEMPHIS AND FORT SMITH.**

So... Exactly where did the stagecoaches of Butterfield stop 508 times in Lewisburg for fresh horses between September 1858 and March 1861?

With these clues that the *'Markham Tavern'* might be the answer to our quest, this enabled a more focused search instead of the vague "stage stop" or "livery."

APRIL 2, 2024
THE 3RD SOLID CLUE

In the *"Historical Marker Database,"* for the 'Historic Moose House,' it refers to the Markham Tavern as:
"AN OLD STAGE STOP IN LEWISBURG..."

APRIL 2, 2024
THE 4TH SOLID CLUE

An on-line post by the Honors College of the University of Central Arkansas article entitled, 'Lewisburg,' states:

*"MARKHAM TAVERN served as a **RELAY STATION ON THE BUTTERFIELD ROUTE** between Little Rock and Fort Smith..."*

APRIL 2, 2024
THE 5TH SOLID CLUE

On the May 15, 1974 nomination form to the National Register of Historic Places (15-57-M295-61), concerning the Moose House at 711 Green Street in Morrilton, the following two photographs were included along with the statement:

"Moose house ... from the Markham Tavern, **AN OLD STAGE STOP IN LEWISBURG**...*"*

Moose House in 1974, at 711 Green Street, Morrilton, AR
The front portico has been added to the Markham Tavern structure.

Some years after its relocation to Morrilton in 1866, the structure was *"enlarged and enhanced,"* adding substantially to the rear of the original Markham Tavern building.

April 2, 2024
Markham Tavern & Butterfield Stage Station

The five clues above combine to form a certainty that the name of the stage station used by the Butterfield stagecoaches at Lewisburg is indeed "MARKHAM TAVERN."

The Markham Tavern was originally built by Reuben T. Markham, close to the banks of the Arkansas River in the community of Lewisburg about 1832.

The Markham Tavern is a 2½ story wood frame structure with a gable roof and weatherboard siding.

In reply to my request for information on the "*Remember Morrilton*" Facebook page, Steve Beavers **revealed that the structure still existed**! He reported that some time after the Civil War, James Miles Moose moved the tavern north about a mile to the new community of Morrilton. A few years later, when the railroad tracks were laid, many of the Lewisburg residents also moved about a mile north of the Lewisburg river port to locate along the newly installed railroad.

Steve Beavers wrote, "*Several years ago, a group from the museum traveled to the area and found the probable location of the Markham Tavern. The rock foundations, a cistern, and the well was located. This is located on private property and I would not recommend visiting without permission of the landowners.*

The Markham Tavern was moved and used to build the core of the Moose House. When the Moose family still owned the home, I was given a tour and allowed to take photos. Portions of the old tavern were still visible throughout the home. Once I have some down time, I will look up those photos and share them. There was also a virtual tour put together using the photos I took that day."

Julie Taylor echoed the comment of Steve Beavers concerning the Moose house when she posted on Remember Morrilton, "The Markham Tavern was moved to Morrilton in the 1860's by James Moose. It's known as the Moose House now, **AND IS STILL STANDING.**"

When James Miles Moose completed his service in the Confederate Army, he left his duty station in Texas and returned to Conway County, Arkansas. When he discovered that his former home had been burned during the recent war, he decided to rebuild on the same lot.

He obtained the Markham Tavern, located one mile south in Lewisburg. He relocated the old stagecoach stop north to 711 Green Street, for use as his new home.

James and Sophia Moose had ten children, one of whom became president of the Arkansas Senate and a judge in the 5th District of Arkansas. Their youngest son, James Sayle Moose, was born 1875 in the Moose House. This youngest son lived in that home 78 years until his death. His son, James Sayle Moose Jr., former U. S. Ambassador to several middle eastern countries, became owner in the home and lived there many years.

Markham Tavern / Moose House 2024
Photo by Carmel Inc.

When the home was 190 years old, it was put on the market for sale. The three bedroom, three bath, 3,776 sq foot home sold for $438,000 on June 1, 2022.

Butterfield Overland National Historic Trail Through Arkansas' Pope & Conway Counties

Markham Tavern & Butterfield Stage Station

This photo was taken after James Miles Moose *"reconstructed"* the Markham Tavern *"log by log and plank by plank"* one mile north on 711 Green Street in Morrilton in 1866. After photo was taken, Moose *"enlarged and enhanced"* the tavern. This structure was originally built about 1835 by Reuben T. Markham, close to the banks of the Arkansas River in the community of Lewisburg.

Photo courtesy of the Morrilton's Conway County Museum

Some years after the above photo was made, the structure was *"enlarged and enhanced,"* adding a two-story portico entrance and rooms in the rear of the home.

Moose House/Markham Tavern Scene
*This image, perhaps ca. 1900, shows the Moose House in the snow with the Morrilton Male and Female College behind the house.
Photo courtesy of the Conway County History Museum*

"Old Lewisburg, Ark." a Grissom Photo
Arrow is pointing to the town at left. The river bank is on the right.
Source: Euna Beavers

Foundation Stones near the Markham Tavern Butterfield Station
The Morrilton Historical Society explored the old Lewisburg site, and discovered these foundation stones near the former site of the Butterfield stage station at Reuben T. Markham's Tavern in Lewisburg, Arkansas. Image courtesy of Euna Beavers, Morrilton Historical Society

Old Cistern near the Markham Tavern Butterfield Station
This cistern serviced one of the businesses or homes in downtown Lewisburg. Image courtesy of Euna Beavers, Morrilton Historical Society

Well or Cistern near the old Butterfield Station in Lewisburg
There were two good wells in old Lewisburg. One of those wells was at Butterfield's stage stop station at Markham's Tavern across the road from the Gordon home. Image courtesy of Euna Beavers, Morrilton Historical Society

This 200 Year old magnolia tree is still standing at the Gordon home site across the street from the old Butterfield Station site at Markham's Tavern in Lewisburg.

Big Jim Bently

While visiting with Margaret Motley at the Potts Inn Museum, she shared with me an article on Lewisburg which included a story of the *'stevedore'* dockworkers.

"Jim Bentley, a dockworker at Lewisburg, carried all the heavy loads up and down the hill. According to Mrs. Isley, the first face to be seen when the steamboat came to town was "Big Jim." Wondrous and fearful tales of Jim's strength have come down to us. **He could lift 900 pounds with ease**, and he was once seen to carry three barrels of salt up the steep grade. No loaders were needed, for Jim handled a bale of cotton with great ease."

When the dockworkers were unloading the steamship, during that hectic rush, they would sing the "tune of some lively river ballad." (*"A Town That Disappeared: Lewisburg, Arkansas," by Nina McReynolds, 1958, page 5.0*

APRIL 2, 2024

While assisting Dr. John Fahey search for post offices along the Butterfield Overland National Trail in Benton County, Arkansas I discovered a map drawn by James L. Lucas of Plumer's Station, in February 13, 1873.

The map accompanied a Post Office Department form requesting the establishment of a post office near the home of Samuel Plummer, Butterfield station agent. The form required that a map be included to indicate the proposed location in relationship to existing post offices nearby.

For a title on the map, Mr. Lucas wrote:
Map of Conway County
Remarks
Lewisburg Post Office distance form Plumers Station - 8 miles.
Springfield P.O. distance from Plumers Station - 11 miles.
Conway Station P.O. distance from Plumer's Station - 14 miles.

Butterfield Overland National Historic Trail Through Arkansas' Pope & Conway Counties

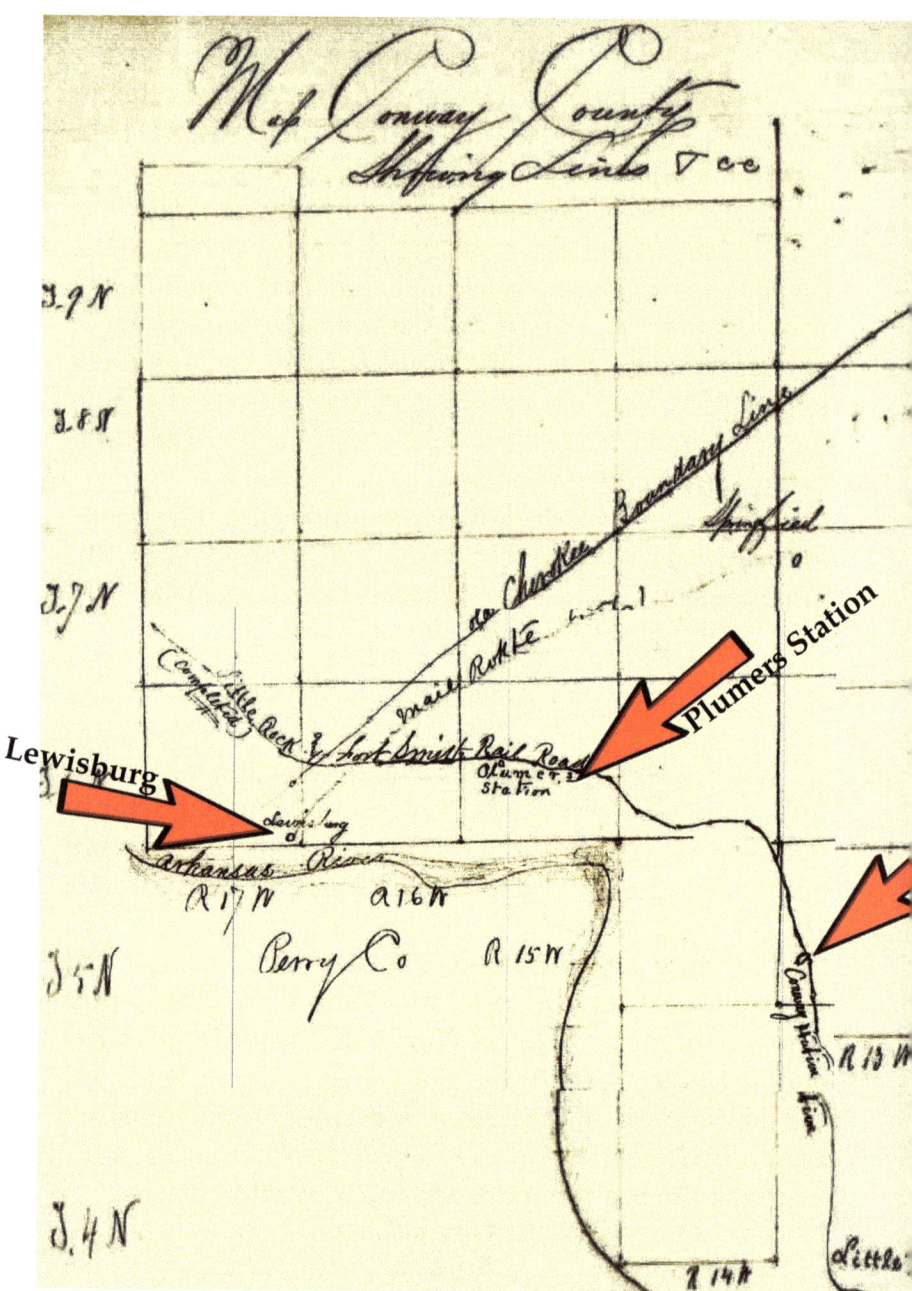

SOURCE: "Post Office Reports of Site Locations, 1837–1950" located at The National Archives Building in Washington, DC, on microfilm roll 27 including "Arkansas Cleveland to Craighead Counties, page 760

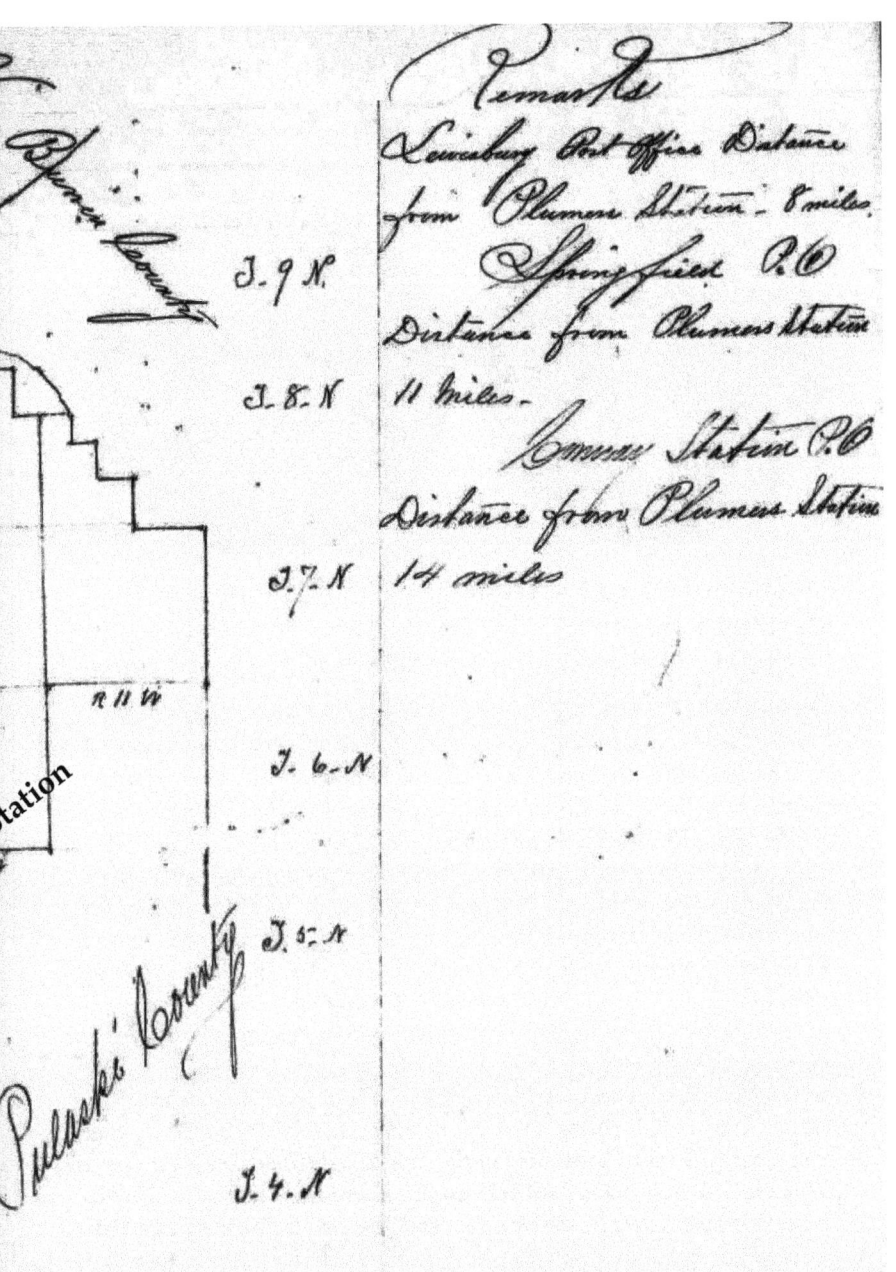

Map by James L. Lucas of Plumer's Station, February 13, 1873.
On line source: https://catalog.archives.gov/id/68200585?objectPage=760

April 6, 2024

Ann Sledge Landers discovered a Markham Tavern token on the Stacks & Bowers auction site.

The token came from Johns Saloon in the R. T. Markham Tavern.

Selling in the auction for $488.75, the auction house described the lot:

"*Arkansas, Conway County. (1861-65) R. T. Markham. Johns Saloon 5¢. F-200A-1a. Fuld Rarity-8. Sharpness of VF, some planchet roughness and old, shallow scratches. Copper. Merchant's information on five lines. Rv. JOHNS curves above, SALOON arcs below, FIVE / CENTS at center, stars flanking. Deep golden brown with some minor disturbances, as noted. This interesting die shows that the word THE was first spelled HHE, with the proper T later stamped over the first H; ATHTHE is plainly evident in the die. A rare token from the Arkansas series.*

The 1860 Census for Conway County, Arkansas included a 35-year-old male named Ruben T. Markham who worked as a hotel keeper. Markham appears to have originally been from Alabama. Jeff LeMaster in an article titled "Door to the Past, History of Lewisburg to be celebrated Saturday" published in the May 10, 2007 edition of Arkansas Democrat-Gazette noted: "**Markham Tavern** ... *was a rest stop for river travelers and a* **stagecoach relay station on the Butterfield Trail** *between Memphis and Fort Smith. The tavern served such travelers as famous Texan Sam Houston and was owned by Ruben T. Markham"*

Provenance: From the Alan Bleviss Collection of Civil War Tokens; purchased from Steve Tanenbaum.

April 20, 2024

On a sunny Saturday afternoon, Marcia and I made another trip to the Conway County History Museum, searching for more information, now that we knew the Markham Tavern was the Butterfield stage station.

Concerning the Markham Tavern, several references to the Tavern's relocation were found in the Conway County History Museum's library: *"Conway County - Our Land, Our Home, Our People,"* compiled by the Conway County Historical Society, 2nd edition, 1992:

"James Miles Moose, March 21, 1827, and Sophia Emily Stockton, June 6, 1833, were married in Lewisburg, March 21, 1853, and moved to Morrilton in 1866 where they raised their family in the Green Street home made from the Lewisburg tavern." (page 388, submitted by May Hope Moose)

Sophia Emily (Stockton) Moose and James Miles Moose

"When he returned from the war, he purchased in 1866, the **Markham Tavern in Lewisburg and** *had it RECONSTRUCTED on Green Street in Morrilton.*

The logs held together with square pegs (still visible today), the house was enlarged and enhanced until it became one of the finest homes in the city. It is on the National Register of Historic Homes. Members of the family still own it and live there." ("Conway County - Our Land, Our Home, Our People," compiled by the Conway County Historical Society, 2nd edition, 1992, page 389 submitted by May Hope Moose)

The Conway County History Museum has on display a photograph of the old Markham Tavern before it was *"enlarged and enhanced"* by the Moose family.

The Markham Tavern
This photo was taken after James Moose "reconstructed" the Markham Tavern, but before it was 'enlarged and enhanced" adding a two-story portico in front.

The Markham Tavern / Moose Home *after it was "enlarged and enhanced. At the time of this photo in 1989, the Moose House was owned by Edward Beamon Howell, Jr., a great-great-grandson of James Miles Moose who bought and reconstructed the Markham Tavern in 1866.*

Bill Holt, the volunteer at the museum, provided an article on Lewisburg written by Arkansas Historic Preservation Program:

"The Moose House at 711 Green Street was **built about 1835 in old Lewisburg and was known as the Markham Tavern**.

It stood on the main street of town opposite the Anderson Gordon home. After the Civil War, there were few travelers and a fire damaged the building. When James Miles Moose returned from four year's service with the Confederate troops, he found his home in ruins. Undaunted, **he bought the tavern and moved it, log by log, and plank by plank, to its present location.**

The house reflects the continuing influence of the Greek Revival style, but in transition toward the French Second Empire style, as evidenced by the two-story portico projecting out beyond the pediment above to create a visually separate component. Nevertheless, its horizontal weather boarding and symmetrical six-over-six sash windows recall the grandeur of larger antebellum homes. Members of the Moose family still own it." (*Arkansas Historic Preservation Program*)

The Markham Tavern /*Moose Home as it appears in 2023.*
Photo by Duane and Tracy Marsteller, October 15, 2023

Leaving Lewisburg

Leaving Lewisburg, the stagecoach crossed Point Remove Creek on the way westward to Hurricane Station. In the 1830's the Point Remove Creek ferry was owned by William Ellis, father-in-law to Samuel Plummer.

Concerning Point Remove Creek, in about 1825 a survey was conducted for the proposed Military Road between Little Rock and Fort Gibson. The surveyor's notes contain the following statement when he reached 156 miles from Fort Gibson: *"Point Remove creek —country gently rolling, part level, some low grounds; a causeway of a few yards will be required in one place, across a cypress swamp; timber, oak, gum, ash, hickory & c. A bridge will be required across this creek, which will cost about $300, or a ferry may be established by bestowing considerable labor in improving the landing."*

The surveyors observations proved correct. Within a decade William Ellis owned a 60 foot ferry that he placed on Point Remove Creek. In dry weather the Ellis Ferry served as a stationary bridge over the creek. In seasons of high water, the Ellis Ferry was put into service carrying people, livestock, and wagons over the full and raging waters. [Source: Carolyn Yancey Kent's paper, "Samuel Plummer (1800-1876)."]

It is not known if the Ellis Ferry was still in service between 1858 and 1861 for the Butterfield stagecoaches to cross Point Remove Creek. Due to the size and nature of Point Remove Creek, the Ellis Ferry or its replacement was surely put to use as the Butterfield stagecoaches left Conway County and headed west for the Pope County stations at Hurricane, Kirkbride Potts, Norristown's Dardanelle Ferry and on west to Stinnet Station, Shoal Creek and Fort Smith.

My wife's family lived on the Butterfield Route between the Markham and Hurricane Stations

Swain's Store at Blackwell
My wife's grandfather lived along the railroad tracks parallel to the old Butterfield Trail. Sherman N. "Sam" Swain was the postmaster, and owner of the Swain Store in Blackwell. Opening in 1928, the store sold groceries, livestock feed, canned goods, and the basic necessities.

Butterfield National Historic Trail at Blackwell
The trail passes through the community of Blackwell, halfway between the Markham (Lewisburg) and Hurricane (Atkins) Stations, just 1/2 mile from the Swain Store.

My wife's family lived on the Butterfield Route between the Markham and Hurricane Stations

The Swain Family
Sherman Norton Swain with grandchildren Olivia Smirl, Sherry Swain and Marcia Swain.

Marcia Swain, at age 19 married Bob Crossman. They live in Conway and have two sons and five grandchildren.

The Swain Family
All of the children of Sam and Stella were raised along the railroad tracks that were laid parallel to the Butterfield Trail.
From left to right" Ansel Swain, Doyle Swain, Dallas Swain, Sam Swain holding Joe Smirl, Stella Swain, Allene Swain Smirl, and Shirley Swain.

Butterfield Overland National Historic Trail Through Arkansas' Pope & Conway Counties

Pope County

BUTTERFIELD OVERLAND NATIONAL HISTORIC TRAIL THROUGH POPE COUNTY, ARKANSAS

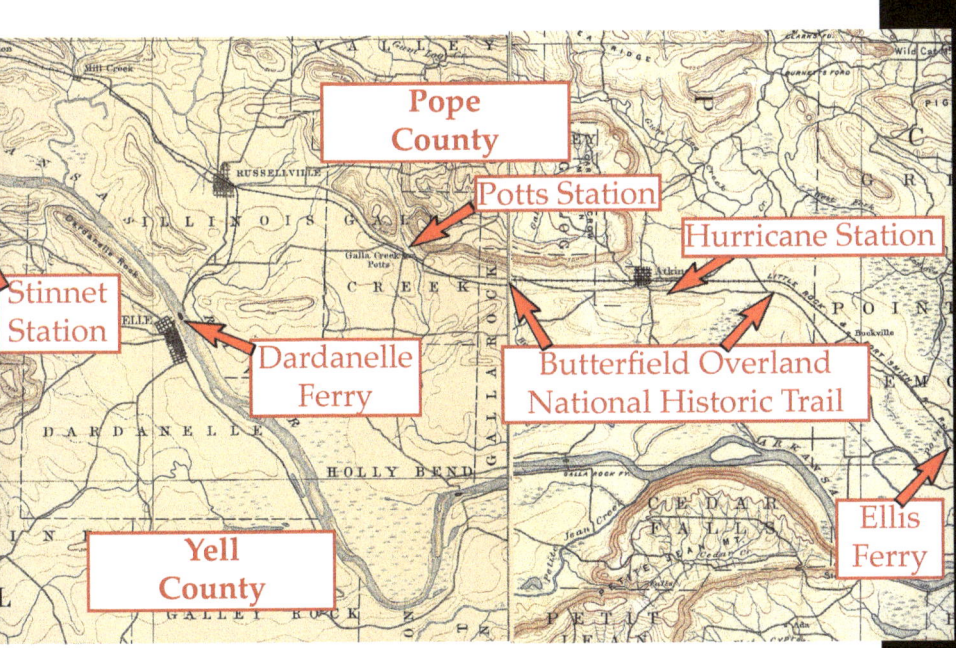

1888 Topographical Map, USGS, Henry Gannett chief geographer, topography by H. B. Blair from 1888 survey.

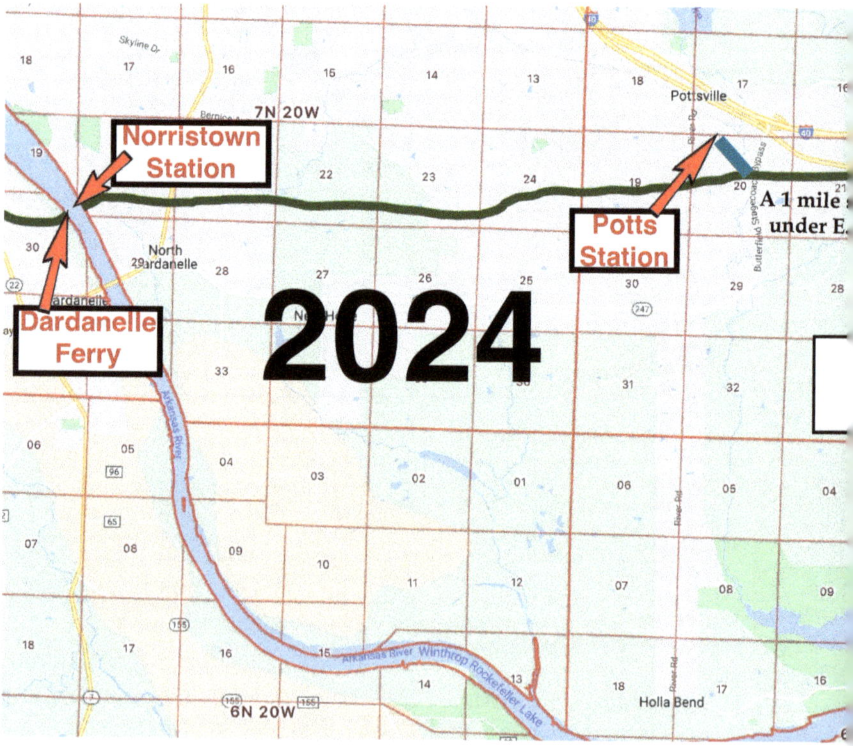

Butterfield Overland National Historic Trail Through Arkansas' Pope & Conway Counties

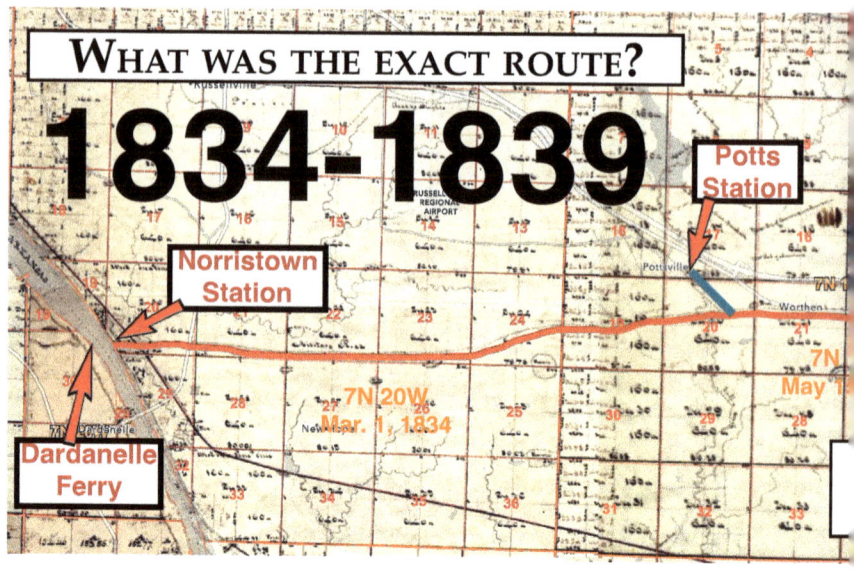

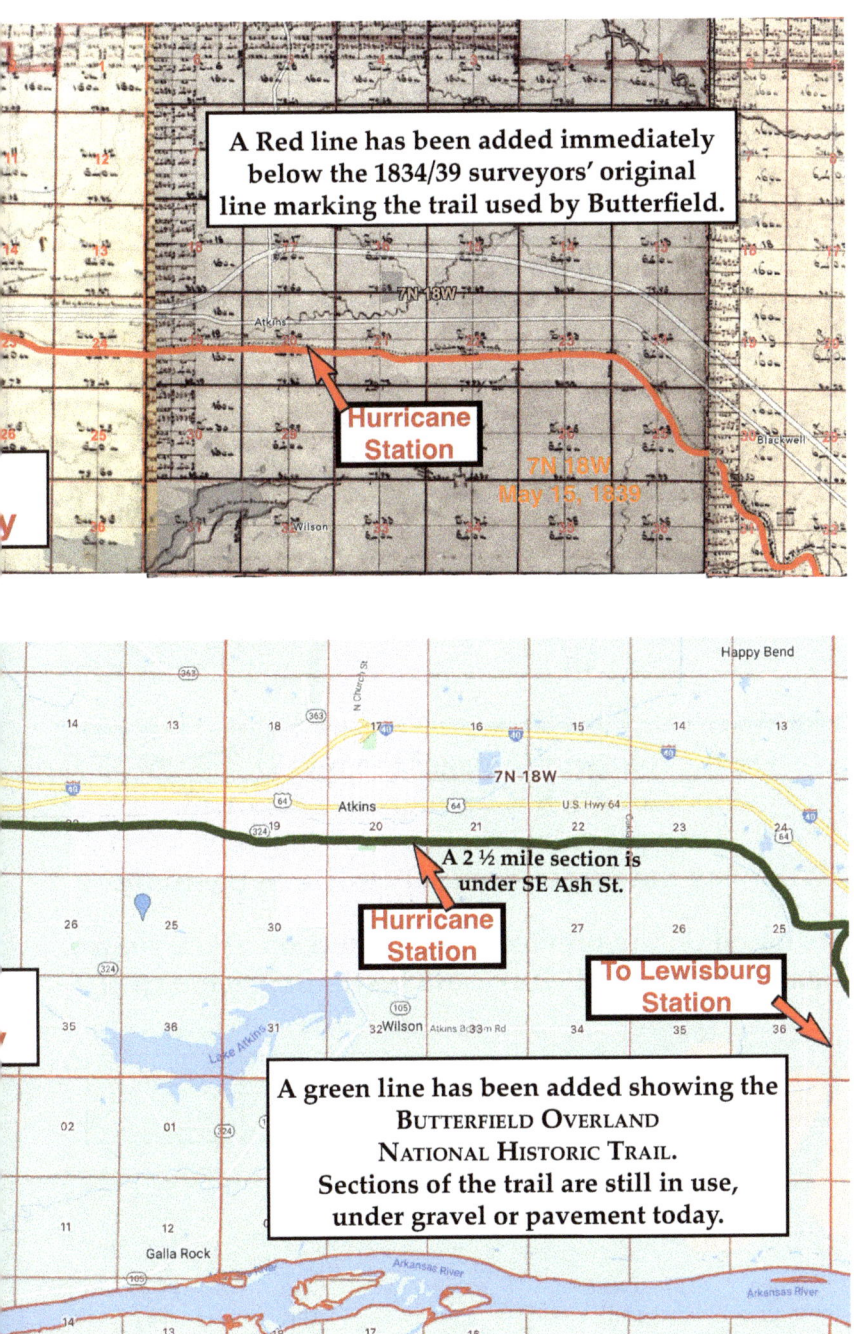

Butterfield Overland National Historic Trail Through Arkansas' Pope & Conway Counties

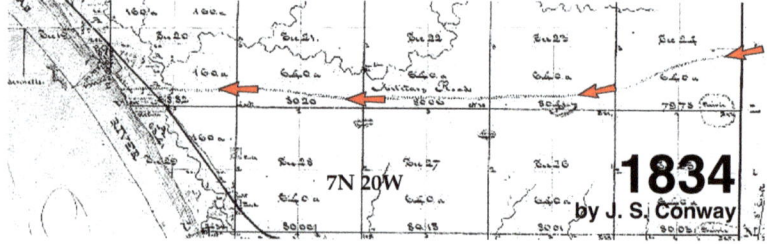

Comparing the survey above with the one below,
reveals that between March 1, 1834 and 1869,
the route of the Old Military Road
between Norristown and Potts Inn did not change.
The 1834 survey above, compliments of the Bureau of Land Management.
1869 Robinson survey below, compliments of the Faulkner County Museum

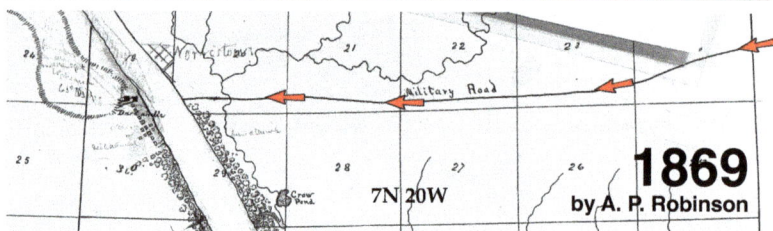

On the following 5 pages, the route through
Pope County has been greatly enlarged.
They piece together as shown below,
allowing the reader to closely examine the route.

As noted on the previous page, a section of the route near Potts Inn and Hurricane is still in use today.

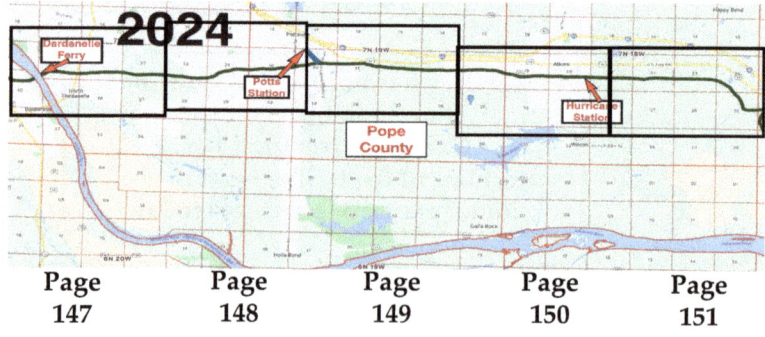

| Page 147 | Page 148 | Page 149 | Page 150 | Page 151 |

— 150 —
© 2024 Robert O. Crossman

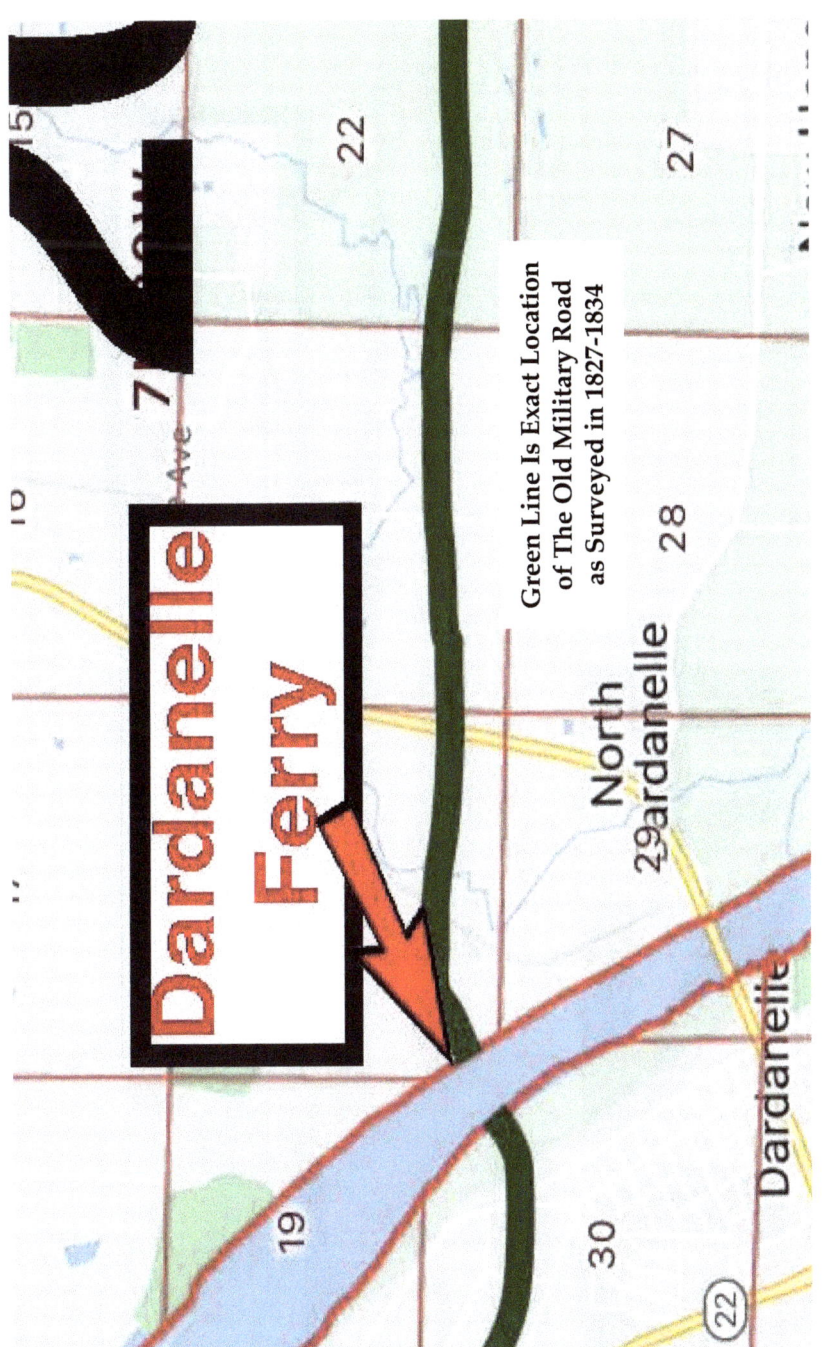

Butterfield Overland National Historic Trail Through Arkansas' Pope & Conway Counties

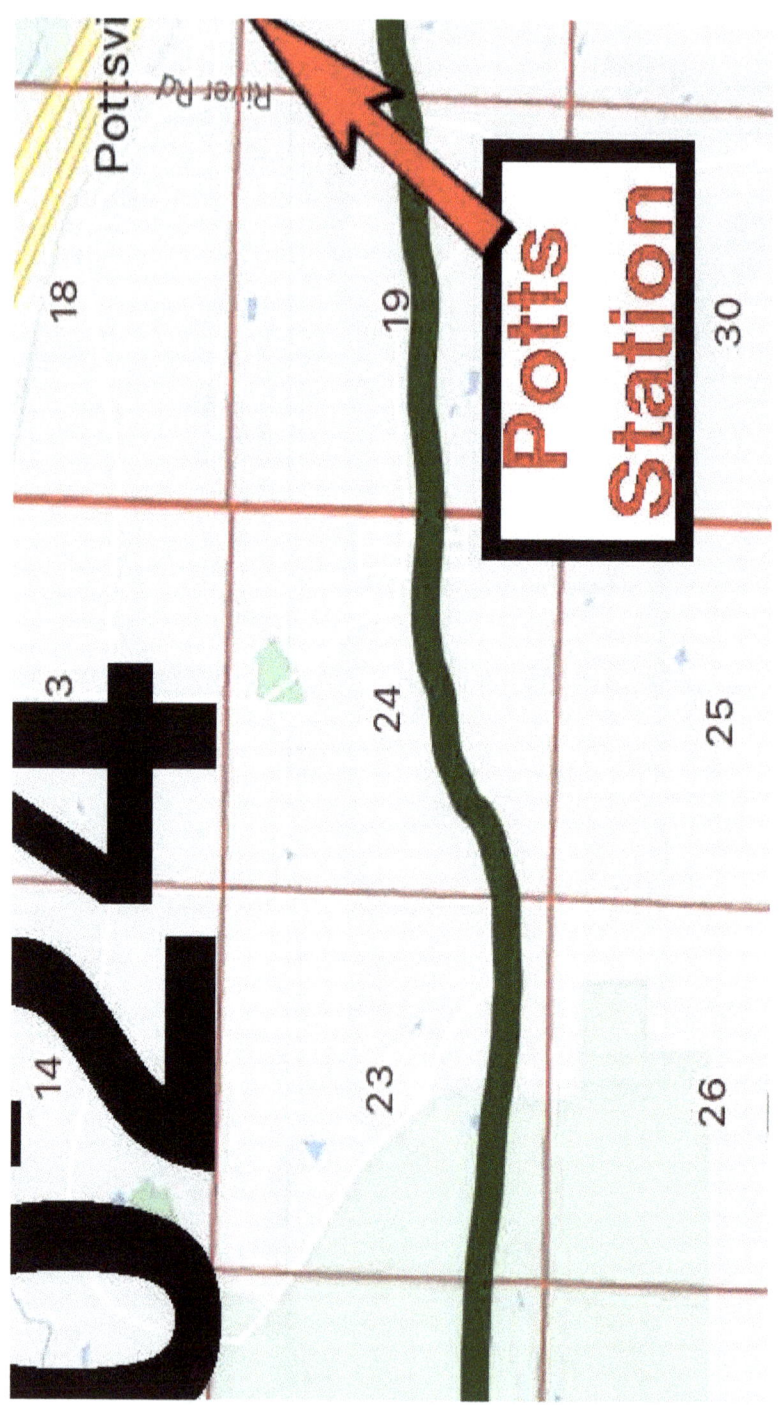

Butterfield Overland National Historic Trail Through Arkansas' Pope & Conway Counties

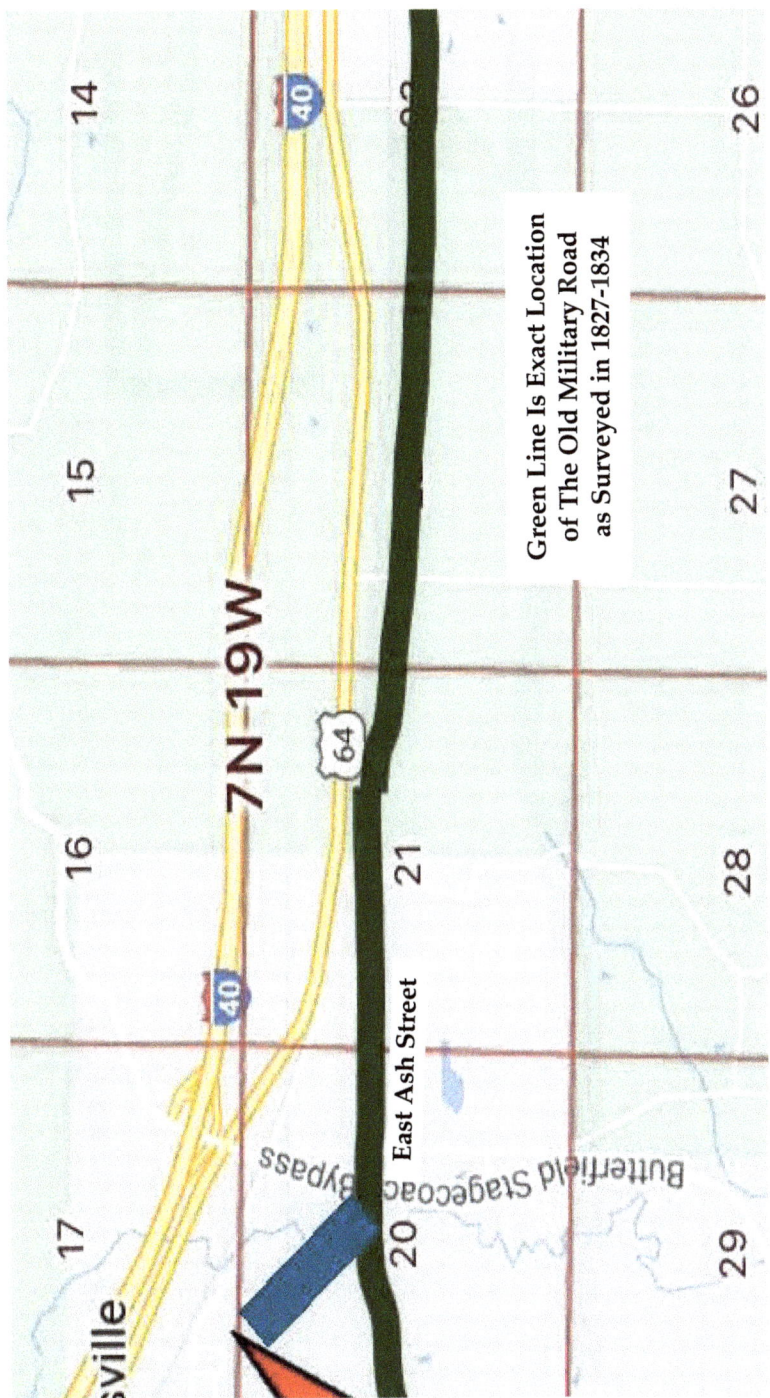

Butterfield Overland National Historic Trail Through Arkansas' Pope & Conway Counties

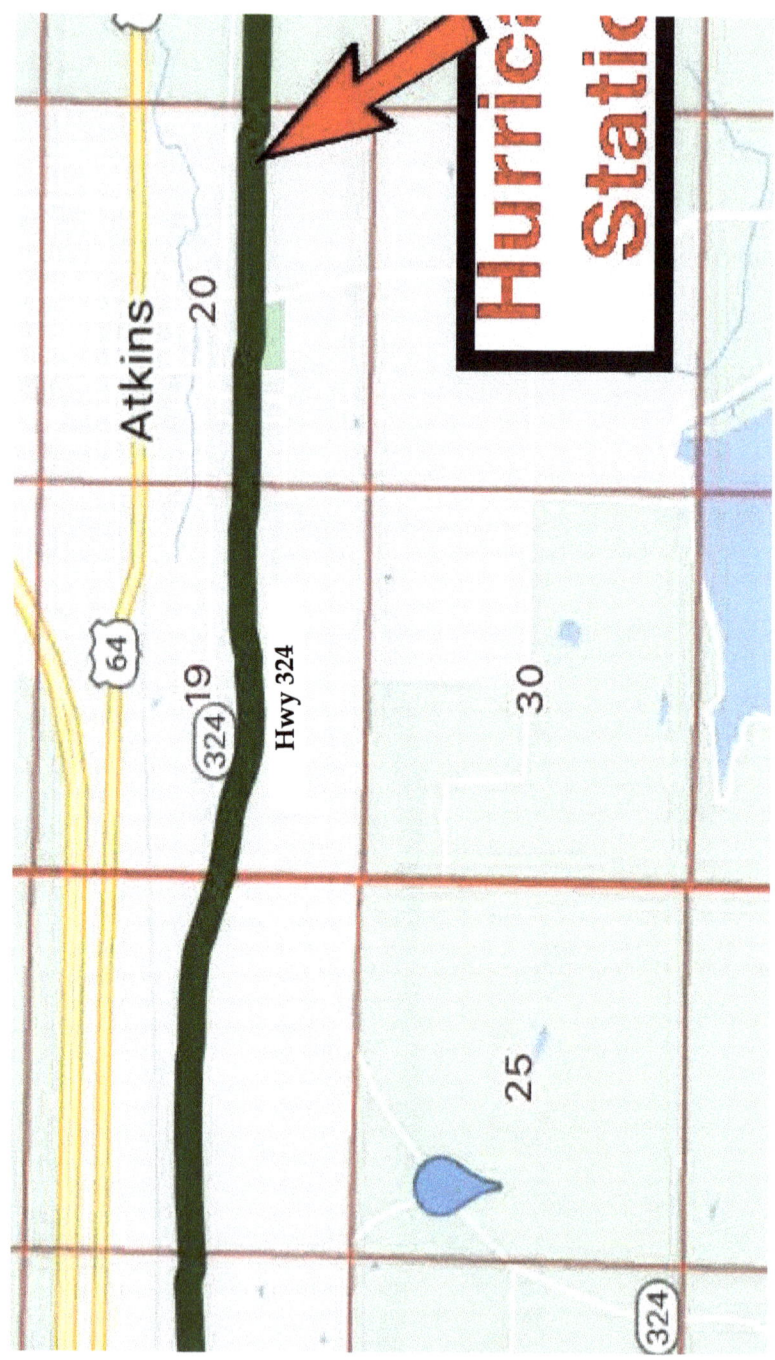

Butterfield Overland National Historic Trail Through Arkansas' Pope & Conway Counties

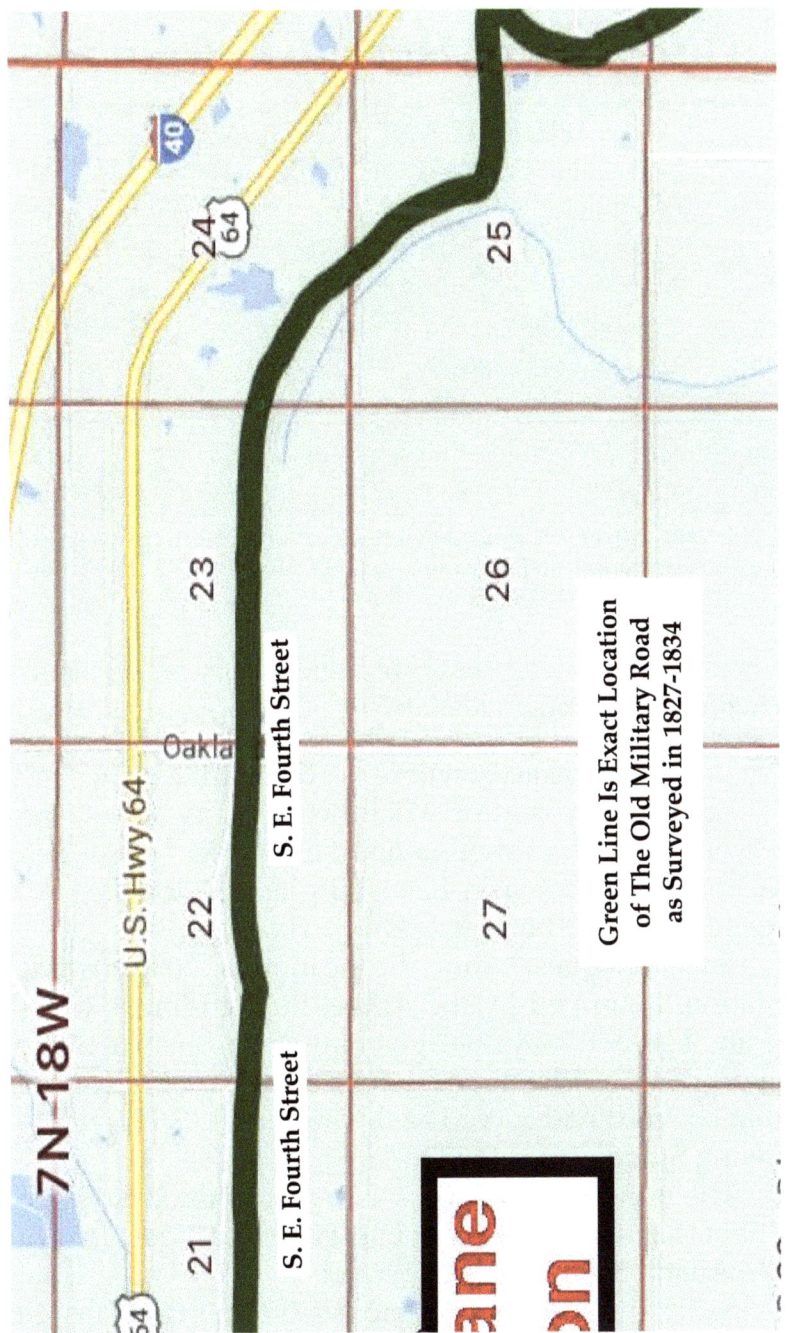

Discovery of Hurricane Station

HURRICANE STATION
N 35.237352, W -92.903704

This 1852 map of Arkansas shows the location of Hurricane west of Lewisburg Station, and nine miles east of Galla Creek's Potts Station.
1852 Map of Arkansas, by D. F. Shall, Little Rock Surveyors Office

---

"From Lewisburg the stage route was by way of **Hurricane***, Potts Station, to Norristown."* "The Butterfield Overland Mail in Arkansas," by W. J. Lemke and Ted R. Worley, 1957, page 15

So, exactly where is Hurricane?

I'd lived in central Arkansas for fifty years, but never heard of a town named Hurricane. Lemke and Worley list it between Lewisburg and Pottsville, so I decided it must be near Atkins, Arkansas.

In a 2019 quest to find the location of the Hurricane Station, I stopped by the Atkins Public Library to inquire. Gaynell Hays-Steaggs happened be next to me at the counter. She directed me to a one story red stable that she said had served as the Butterfield's Hurricane Swing Station from 1858 to 1861.

The building stood on a dirt road named S. E. 4th Street, formerly known as Old Wire Road, just east of the Austin School Crossing Road.

Sadly, the stable was demolished four years later, in 2023.

Posting an inquiry on the *"Atkins, Arkansas Memories"* and *"Backroads of Arkansas"* Facebook page resulted in dozens of replies, including the following:
- Bradley Harris reported that his grandmother lives just 200 yards west of the red building. *(see photo on the following page)* Bradley's grandmother grew up hearing the story and knowing that this was indeed the swing station of the Butterfield Overland Stage from 1858 to 1861.
- This was confirmed as the original stage station by Dena Gray's reply, whose father Dean Freeman owns the property and lives in a home across the street.
- Lucky Gipson reported that the property was previously owned by his uncle, Mr. Freeman's father-in-law, Neil Carnell Gipson. Lucky Gipson also revealed that a small cemetery is still located in the woods northeast of the barn.
- Todd Brock informed me that there is a historical Butterfield plaque to the west of this location near the 4th street and Hwy. 105 intersection. *(see photo below)*

Hurricane Historical Marker

This historical marker is on the same road west of the Hurricane site above, was placed during the Atkins Bicentennial Celebration in 1976.

Hurricane Station
This is the building that the current property owners and neighbors have always been told served as a Swing Station for the Butterfield Overland Mail Co. Sadly, this building was demolished in 2023.

Hurricane Butterfield Station
On S. E. 4th Street, just east of Union Grove/Austin School road. The larger gambrel roof red barn behind the swing station was built some years after the Butterfield stage stopped running.

Hurricane, Arkansas Historical References

There is a map of Arkansas published in 1852 by "D. H. Shall, late principal clerk of the Surveyor's Office at Little Rock" that shows the location of Hurricane to be north of the Arkansas river between Lewisburg (present day Morrilton) and Galla Creek (present day Pottsville) on the Old Military/ Wire Road.

The "Hurricane P.O." and "Galley C. P.O." are also shown on the 1864 Arkansas map by Helmuth Holtz shown below.

1864 Map of Arkansas and Louisiana by Helmuth Holtz
Showing the location of "Hurricane P.O." west of Lewisburg Station, and nine miles east of Galley Creek P.O. at Potts Station.

We know that a post office existed at Hurricane, east of Potts Inn. In the 1840's when Kirkbride Potts was the postmaster of Galley Creek (Pottsville, AR) he had to fill out and personally sign a form for the Post Master General.

"Site Location Reports of Post Offices, 1837-1950," on microfilm at the Arkansas State Archives, Little Rock, catalog # MG02116 AHC

On that 1840's form we read, *"The name of the nearest office on the same route on the other side is <u>Hurricane</u> and its distance is <u>9</u> miles in a <u>East</u> direction from it."*

While Butterfield's Overland carried mail across the continent, mail still needed to be carried from village to village. By 1851 the U.S. Post Office had divided Arkansas into 110 routes and delivered mail to about 350 post offices by horseback, carriage and wagon.

We do not have the names of the Hurricane postmasters from the Butterfield's Overland time frame of 1858-1861, however the postmasters for 1851 are known. The *"1851 Post Office Guide"* list the post masters names for several locations that would later have a Butterfield connection including: Cadron - John W. Gilbert; Lewisburg - Gordon Anderson; Gally Creek - Kirkbride Potts; Norristown - Thomas A. Howell and Hurricane - Stephen D. Lewis. Kara Bower has noted that Postmaster Stephen D. Lewis, husband of Lydia Barnes Potts, was the brother-in-law of Kirkbride Potts.

Early Postal Routes That Include Hurricane

In 1851, U.S. Postal Route #5904 left Little Rock direct to Lewisburg, Hurricane, Galley Creek, Norristown, Dwight, and Scottia, to Pittsburg. Mail would leave Little Rock at 2 p.m. every Monday and Friday, arriving at Pittsburg by 12 p.m. next days. Then leaving Pittsburg at 10 a.m. every Tuesday and Saturday, arriving at Little Rock by 8 p.m. next days.

Nearby in 1851 another Route #5907 left Little Rock direct to Cadron, Quitman, to Kinderhook. Mail would leave Little Rock at 5 a.m. every Thursday, arrive at Kinderhook by 7 p. m., next day. Then leaving Kinderhook at 5 a.m, every Tuesday, arrive at Little Rock by 7 p.m. next day.

"The United States Post-Office Guide," by Eli Bowen, D. Appleton and Company, New-York, 200 Broadway, 1851, pgs. 169, 170, and 331

So, it is confirmed that Hurricane existed on the Old Wire Road, and that Butterfield's Overland Mail

Co. stage passed by the building. Also we have confirmed that Hurricane was indeed a post office in the 1840's to 1860's with Stephen D. Lewis as postmaster.

Butterfield Trail Near Hurricane Station
Photo by Margaret Motley Feb 2021, Overland Mail route near Hurricane.

Looking at this 2021 photo by Margaret Motley, if you listen carefully you can almost hear the rumble of the Butterfield Overland Mail Stage as it traveled over this original route near Hurricane on the 1828 Old Military / Wire Road.

Hurricane Station by Atkins, Arkansas artist Nina Richardson
with Carrion Crow Mountain in the distance.
Image of original painting from the collection of Bill Swain of Atkins

1847 Letter From Hurricane, Arkansas

What may be the only surviving letter from Hurricane, Arkansas is shown below. The letter was written by the Hurricane Postmaster Stephen D. Lewis, and his wife Lydia Potts Lewis. She is the daughter of Kirkbride Potts, Butterfield station agent and postmaster nine miles to the west in Galla Creek, Arkansas.

> Hurricane Conway Co Arks
> May 29 1847
>
> Dear Sister I take this opportunity of communicating to you by our neice Sarah Potts She was down to see me a few days ago She will give you all the particulars of my situation I have written to you a few mails ago which I hope you have receved before this time we are all well except my self I feel some what unwell this morning with I hope nothing more than a bad head ache we are this day cutting our wheat it is considered verry good I have nothing of importance to write as Sarah will tell you all about our country our season have been verry cool, rather uncomfortable for the season of the year
>
> I sincerly wish you would consent to come to Arks with Sarah when she returns. Excuse me my Dear Sister for so short a letter at the same time you may rest assured this is from one who feels as great an interest for you and your welfare as any other living Creature on this earth adieu my Dear sister for a while, Pleas write as soon as Sally gets them and dont fail as I wish to hear from you verry much and often
>
> Stephen D Lewis
> Lydia B Lewis
>
> Dear Sister
> I send you this small present as it consumes no room you must get you a dress

Transcription is on the following page.

Hurricane, Conway Co., Ark.
May 29, 1847

Dear Sister,

    I take this opportunity of communicating to you by our niece Sarah Potts. She was down to see me a few days ago. She will give you all the particulars of my situation.

    I have written to you a few weeks ago which I hope you have read before this time. We are all well except for myself. I feel somewhat unwell this morning which I hope nothing more than a bad headache.

    We are this day cutting down our wheat. It is considered very good.

    I have nothing of importance to write as Sarah will tell you all about our country. Our season has been very cool rather uncomfortable for the season of the year.

    I sincerely wish you would consent to come to Ark. when Sarah returns. Excuse me my dear sister for so short a letter at the same time you may most assume this is from one who feels as great an interest for you and your welfare as any other living creature on this earth.

    Adieu my Dear Sister for a while.

    Please write as soon as Sally gets there and don't fail as I wish to hear from you very much and often.

Dear Sister,
I sent you this small present as it consumes no room you must get you a d___.

Stephen D. Lewis
Lydia B. Lewis

Source: Transcription courtesy of Kara Bowers, Potts Inn Museum. Image of letter courtesy of the Arkansas State Archives.

This historical marker at the Lewisburg Cemetery credits Stephen D. Lewis (see his signature on the letter above) for founding the first Trading Post of Conway County at Lewisburg, Arkansas in 1825.

Just two miles northwest of Hurricane, the town of Atkins sprung up along the 1870 railroad tracks, and the community of Hurricane faded away.

Atkins Street Scene, 1878
Courtesy of Arkansas State Archives

Street Scene at Atkins, Looking North on Galla Street, ca. 1890
Courtesy of Arkansas State Archives

My wife's family lived near Hurricane for 60 years.

A. D. Stubbs Store 1901-1912 — W. T. Hamlet & Co. Store 1913-1923
By 1913, brothers Tom, Charley and Turner Hamlet became full owners of the A. D. Stubbs Store in Fowler, Arkansas. The name was later changed to the W. T. Hamlet Store. Upon looking closely at the photo, Turner Hamlet is seen to the left of the door. Look to the left of the photo and you will see a woman standing on the porch of the house. There is a double glider swing near the porch.

W. T. Hamlet & Co. Store 1924-1956, Downtown Atkins
Charlie & Turner Hamlet (my wife's grandfather) seated to the right of the door. In January of 1924, the W. T. Hamlet and Company moved to the downtown in the city of Atkins, Arkansas. (about 1 mile NW of Hurricane) The family also moved to town. The railroad had been built right through the middle of the city. The Hamlet mercantile occupied one of the E. A. Darr Estate buildings on the south side of the railroad track.

My wife's family lived near Hurricane for 60 years.

The Hamlet Brothers
Turner, Tom and Albert

Elizabeth Frances Turner
Moved south of Hurricane in 1859 at the age of three. As a child, Elizabeth likely saw the Butterfield stages pass by.

Elizabeth & John Hamlet
Married at ages 16 and 21 they raised their family south of Hurricane at Galla Rock.

Marriage Certificate
Elizabeth & John Hamlet

Velma & Elizabeth Hamlet
ca. 1924
My wife's grandmother and mother.

Elizabeth Hamlet
My wife's mother was born and raised within one mile of Hurricane.

Hamlet Children, ca. 1900
Tom, Elizabeth (mother), Charley, Albert and Turner

— 166 —
© 2024 Robert O. Crossman

Butterfield Overland National Historic Trail Through Arkansas' Pope & Conway Counties

DISCOVERY OF POTTS STATION
N 35.249582, W -93.046794

"Potts was known as the most hospitable station on the U. S. Stage Line between Little Rock and Fort Smith, and the heart of the weary traveler always bounded with joy when he drew in sight of Potts Station."
The Russellville Democrat, Russellville, Arkansas, Nov. 28, 1878, page 3

"Potts Tavern" by Gloria McHahen, 1984
Print 83 of 500 in Bob Crossman's collection.

Kirkbride Potts, postmaster and station agent, built this home in 1858 for his family. This building also served as an official Butterfield Overland Mail Co. home station. This magnificent structure is open for tours Thursday, Friday and Saturdays 10-3pm in Pottsville, Arkansas.

© 2024 Robert O. Crossman

POTTS STATION
Home of Kirkbride Potts at Galla Creek

Nine miles west of the Hurricane, was a larger "Home Station" known as the Potts Inn, with Kirkbride Potts as station master and postmaster.

Potts Inn is the only surviving Home Station structure in Arkansas. It's a shame that so many of the other Overland Station buildings have faded into history.

At the larger Home Stations, like Potts Inn at Galley Creek, a fresh team was provided. Also, the stagecoach's axles were greased and the passengers could disembark for a quick bite to eat. If the stage was on schedule, passengers were allotted two breaks each day of no more than 40 minutes rest while eating at a Home Station, before reboarding the coach to continue their journey.

Meals cost the passengers from 40¢ to a dollar. At more civilized stations such as the Potts Home Station, passengers came to expect a hearty meal of hot cakes, corn bread, biscuits, pork, fish or wild game, beans, bread, butter, sweet milk and coffee.

For example, at the Fayetteville Home Station, passenger William Tallack reports:

"Our commissariat here amply amends for our recent desert fare. This evening we had a good supper of eggs, honey, potatoes, French beans, steaks and pastry in abundance, and with courtesy; the latter you do not always receive in addition, when in the plains or elsewhere." "The California Overland Express: The Longest Stage Ride in the World," by William Tallack, Historical Society of Southern California, Quarterly Publication, Vol. XVII, Number III, Sept. 1935, pg. 91.

Unlike the great food at the Potts Station, at isolated Overland Stations across the west, fare might be wormy biscuits and grease-laden meat of unknown source.

Kirkbride Potts, Station Agent for Potts Station
Image courtesy of the Potts Inn Museum

The Potts family tells the story that this stepping stone, served as a step for passengers to board the stage four times a week as the stage continued on its journey east to Memphis or west to Fort Smith.

Kara Bowers, Potts Inn and Museum tour guide, Pottsville, Arkansas, during January, 2021 tour.

*Photo by
Bob Crossman
May 2024*

Butterfield Overland National Historic Trail Through Arkansas' Pope & Conway Counties

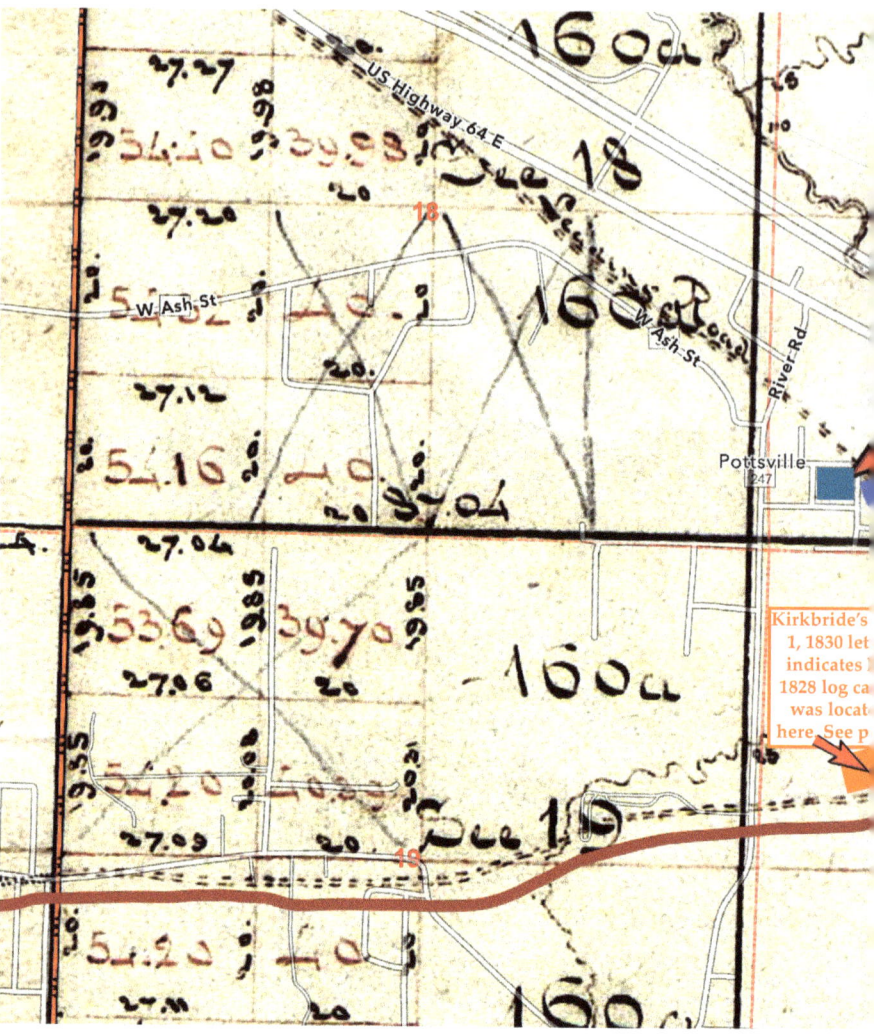

This is a survey from 1827-1834 of the Pottsville, Arkansas area.

The RED line highlights the 1827 Old Military Road that is now called The Butterfield National Historic Trail.

The BLUE line highlights the Dwight Mission Road that served as a spur for the Butterfield stagecoaches to reach Potts Inn.

The arrow points to the POTTS INN Museum- (Pope County Historic Foundation) Pottsville, Arkansas that was a Home Station on the Butterfield Trail.

For reference, in faint background the current roads of today are shown.

Butterfield Overland National Historic Trail Through Arkansas' Pope & Conway Counties

According to this survey, to reach the Potts Inn, the stagecoaches went a very short distance up the 1820 Dwight Mission road. *(Presbyterian mission to the Indians 1820-1829 that was near today's Russellville).* After obtaining fresh horses and a new driver, the stage would go back down that short spur, to continue on the major 1827 road between Memphis and Fort Smith that is marked in red.

Local thought is that the 1827 trail actually ran on the immediate north side of Potts Inn. More research will need to be done with primary sources and LiDAR to determine exactly where the trail crossed through today's Pottsville. Did the historic trail pass on the north or south side of Kirkbride Potts Inn? The 1827 survey indicates that it passed on the south side of Potts Inn.

Potts Inn

We don't have a unique report for conditions at Potts Station. However, an historian wrote that typically:

"At the stage Home Station you would find a stationmaster in charge, a handful of hostlers to care for the animals, and perhaps a rough eating house or restaurant. The buildings would be of logs, whipsawed lumber, sod or adobe, depending on the location. There'd probably be a tin basin on a bench beside the door where you could wash up, aided by some soft soap in a side dish - soap that would curl the hide off a hippo. A roller towel that had seen better days, and a more or less toothless comb, detained by a rawhide string, would help you complete your toilette. Inside there'd be a big fireplace, acid sputtering tallow candles... your meal would be the inevitable hog and hominy or beef and beans of the frontier." 900 Miles on the Butterfield Trail, by A. C. Greene, University of North Texas Press, Denton, Texas, 1994, pg. 23.

The front 'Public Room' was for greeting passengers when the stage arrived at Potts Station in Galley Creek, Arkansas.

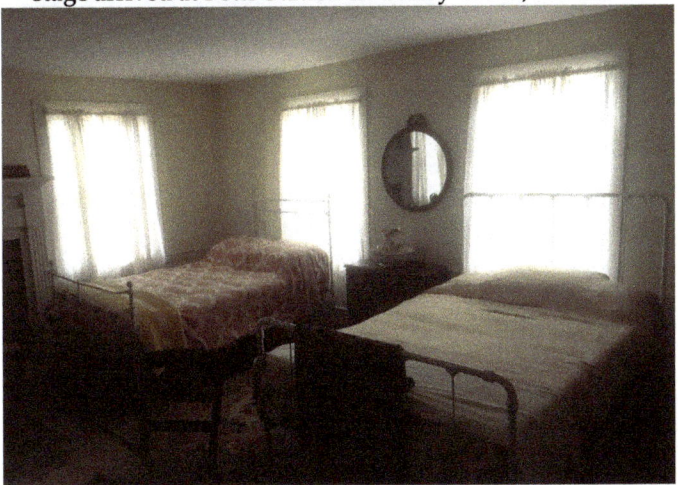

At Potts Station an upstairs room with four beds was available to passengers who wished to debark and spend a night to two, hoping to catch the next stage.

Photos of Potts Inn interior by Bob Crossman, 2020.

    The Overland Mail employees probably had their quarters in an outbuilding on the property. As a Home Station, after completing their 60 mile route, the driver would spend a few nights here at Potts, taking charge of the next stagecoach headed back in the opposite direction. In this way the driver and the horses came to know their 60 mile route so well, they could run the trail even in the dark.

This is the second bedroom on the second floor at Potts Inn.
Photo by Bob Crossman, May 2024

This is the third bedroom on the second floor at Potts Inn.
Photo by Bob Crossman, May 2024

Potts Inn Attic
The spacious attic may have served as "overflow" sleeping quarters when the number of guest exceeded the number of available beds on the second floor.

*Photo by
Bob Crossman
May 2024*

Potts Inn Smoke House, ca 1970
*This structure was restored in the 1970's.
Photo courtesy of Potts Inn Museum*

Kirkbride Potts & The California Gold Rush

Between 1848 and 1857, countless Arkansans had returned from the California Gold Fields, without having achieved the riches they dreamed of. Kirkbride Potts decided to make his fortune by making two trips to California with herds of cattle to sell at lucrative prices to the miners. The *Weekly Arkansas Gazette* on July 25, 1857, published a letter from Kirkbride Potts:

"I have no doubt you will be somewhat surprised at receiving a letter from me, situated as I am, at this time almost on the confines of the State of California, herding a little over three hundred head of cattle. I left my home, in Pope county, on the 22nd of April, 1856, expecting to have returned last winter; but not getting an offer for my stock that I thought would justify for the time, trouble, and expense, I concluded to stay one summer with them and bring them into market this coming fall or winter. They are now in fine order, and will be very fat by November, at which time I hope to meet a good market for them, and return to Arkansas by January, if possible. The crops are very light here this year, owing to the drought...

Beef is down to ten cents on foot, owing to the quantity of Mexican cattle pushed into market. Last winter American beef was 12½ to 13½ on foot, and I think will bear that price again this coming winter. There is not much large America beef in the country: a few thousand head have been driven in from Oregon this spring; but it is doubtful if they get to be good beef by fall. They come in as poor as cattle driven from the States across the plains; and the grass being very short, and pretty much dried up, but few of them will be fit for market the coming fall...

My post office is Red Bluffs. Hoping this may meet your eyes fully restored, I remain yours, Kirkbride Potts."

The profits from his 1849 gold prospecting and two cattle drives allowed Kirkbride Potts to build a rather fabulous home that still stands in Pottsville, Arkansas.

The Witness Tree Standing Between the Kitchen and the Well House

"This Bois D'Arc tree is also known as an Osage Orange, Hedge Apple, or Bow Wood tree. Historically, the wood was used by Native Americans to make strong and resilient bows and arrows. The early settlers also used it to make hubs, spokes, fence posts, and yellow die. Before the advent of barbed wire, living trees were used as fencing. Bois D'Arc trees are dioecious which just means only the females produce fruit. Our tree is a thorn-less male variety that does not produce 'hedge apples/oranges.'

Historical Marker by the witness tree.

In 2021, the Arkansas Department of Agriculture Forestry Devision estimated that the tree started growing in 1790!

When Kirkbride chose this location for his family's new home and Inn, the Bois D'Arc was already 60 years old and probably a large shade tree. It saw the construction of the Potts Inn. It stood fast throughout the Civil War and welcomed community members home after both World Wars. It witnessed the last Potts family members relocate in 1970 and saw the grounds transformed into the museum it is today. Now, you too are a part of this tree's history."

Historical Marker at Potts Inn
(front)

POTTS INN

John Kirkbride Potts (1803-1879) was born in Pennsylvania and moved to Arkansas in the 1820s. In 1828 he settled by Galla Creek, eventually acquiring 650 acres of land. Potts went to California in the Gold Rush of 1849; he failed to strike gold but returned there twice in the early 1850s, driving cattle to feed the miners. With his profits, Potts built this grand home for his large family. Completed in 1858, the house's location on Butterfield's new Overland Mail route made it a convenient stagecoach station and inn for travelers to spend the night. Potts Station also served as a post office with Potts as the postmaster. Pottsville was later named for him.

ARKANSAS HERITAGE

(Continued)

BUTTERFIELD'S OVERLAND MAIL
(Continued from other side)

Needing reliable mail service to California, the U.S. government hired John Butterfield (1801-1869), operator of a stagecoach company in New York, to open an overland route. From 1858, Butterfield's Overland Mail Company delivered mail and passengers by stagecoach and wagon between the Mississippi River and the West Coast in under 25 days. Running via Arkansas, Texas, and New Mexico on its way to California, this 2,800-mile-long southern route avoided snow and was the longest stage line in history. In Arkansas, two branches of the route converged at Fort Smith: a north-south road from St. Louis, Missouri, and an east-west road from Memphis, Tennessee. Butterfield's service on this southern line ended in 1861 due to the onset of the Civil War.

Historical Marker at Potts Inn
(reverse side)

Potts Inn well house.
Photo by Bob Crossman, May 2024

Galla Creek also known as Galley Creek
Photo taken from East Ash Street bridge east of Potts Inn
⅖ mile north of the stagecoach fording location
Various streams from Crow Mountain feed into Galla Creek. Ten miles south of this location, at the community of Galla Rock, Galla Creek flows into the Arkansas River.

Framed Letter hanging in Foyer of Potts Inn.

Courtesy of Potts Inn Museum

Potts Tavern

As the Butterfield stagecoaches came across country from Memphis to Fort Smith, travelers stopped at Inns to eat and sleep. Potts Tavern was a delight to these travel worn people; Potts Tavern being well kept and serving good food.

This Beautiful ante-bellum house was built in the 1850's by Kirkbride Potts. It is now a museum in Pottsville, Ark. It was home for Mr. Potts and his family for many years as well as a stagecoach stop from 1858 to 1861.

Gloria McMahen

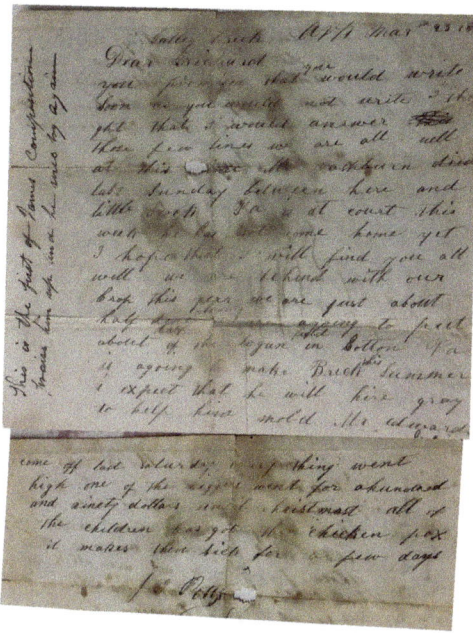

The only known surviving Potts Home Station letter from the Butterfield years.

The Potts Inn Museum has this letter in their collection. It was written in 1860 by one of the sons of Postmaster Kirkbride Potts. It was mailed by James Potts, age 13, to his brother Richard Potts, age 21.

Since it was written and mailed at the Potts Home Station, it was likely carried by Butterfield's Overland Mail coach as it traveled between Memphis and Fort Smith.

Galley Rock March 23 1860

Dear Richard

You promised that you would write soon. As you would not write, I thought that I would answer those few lines. We are all well at this time since M. Washburn died last Sunday between here and Little Rock. Pa is at court this week. He has not come home yet. I hope that I will find you all well. We are behind with our crop this year. We are just about half done plowing where we are going to plant about half of the Logan field in cotton. Pa is going to make brick this summer. Expect that he will hire Gray to help him mold. Mr. Edwards sale come off last Saturday. Every thing went high. One of the nig____s went for a hundred and ninety dollars. Until Christmas all of the children has got the chicken pox. It makes them sick for a few days.   J. J. Potts

Pictured here is the *"Post Desk"* used by Kirkbride Potts, Galla Creek's first postmaster. Kirkbride designed the desk and had it shipped from New Orleans.

All of the local mail, including the Butterfield's Overland Mail Company way mail delivered by the stage coach to Potts Station, was sorted and placed in the owner's slot in this desk. Citizens would come to the Potts Inn Home Station to pick up their mail. *[As you may know, mail was not delivered to each house until 1910 to 1915 in most parts of Arkansas.]*

The desk's doors open to reveal slots for letters, and under the writing surface there is a storage space.

Photo by Bob Crossman, 2024.

Galley Creek Postmaster's Desk

The desk contains an 1847 copy of "Laws and Regulations of the Post Office Department."

Potts was appointed postmaster of Galley Creek (*sometimes called Gally Creek or Galla Creek*) by the president of the United States. Butterfield Overland Mail addressed to Galley Creek or Galla Rock (*actually on the banks of the Arkansas River seven miles to the southeast*), was delivered to postmaster Kirkbride Potts at his home. That mail was handled in the living room using a desk that Potts had ordered from New Orleans.

The form pictured below with Kirkbride Potts signature is an official form he had to fill out in the 1840's for the Postmaster General. The form describes the location of the Galley Creek Post Office in relation to the Hurricane, Norristown and Dover post offices nearby.

"Site Location Reports of Post Offices, 1837-1950," on microfilm at the Arkansas State Archives, Little Rock, catalog # MG02116 AHC

Kirkbride's Choice of Galla Creek

In 1828, a treaty removed the Cherokee from their reservation land *(including the area now called Pottsville)*, and Kirkbride Potts moved into the vacated land that year. Arriving at the age of 25, he first lived at the Arkansas river port known as Galla Rock. Shortly afterward, Potts moved north about 7 miles to an area fed by the waters of Galley Creek running off Crow Mountain. Potts bought 160 acres from the government for 25¢ an acre, and later enlarged his holdings to 720 acres.

In 1828, he chose a high spot on that land at the foot of Crow Mountain near Galley *(or Galla)* Creek and had his enslaved workers build a two-story log house in 1828 for his growing family. In 1858, about a mile south of the log house, he built a grander house where Potts descendants lived until 1970 when they sold it to the Pope County Historical Foundation. "Kirkbride Potts," Encyclopedia of Arkansas, *https://encyclopediaofarkansas.net/entries/john-kirkbride-potts-78*

Potts Inn is Restored
by Faune Conner, Department of Parks and Tourism
Baxter Bulletin (Mountain Home, Arkansas) · 21 Jun 1973, Thu · Page 25

"Standing in the midst of downtown Pottsville is a dignified, 123 year old structure known as Potts Inn. The Inn has recently been restored by the Pope County Historical Foundation as a public attraction. Not merely another antebellum building, the restoration of Potts Inn also resurrects a colorful era in Arkansas history.

Built in 1850-1858, Potts Inn in its heyday was an important stagecoach station on the Butterfield Stage Line which ran between St. Louis and San Francisco. It also served as a regional post office and meeting place for prominent figures and was 'the' place to stay overnight on trips between Little Rock and Fort Smith. The Inn was the stately home of pioneer Kirkbride Potts, and it was his descendants who lived in the house until 1971 when the historical foundation purchased it...

Potts Inn occupies an entire city block, or roughly four acres in the heart of Pottsville. The two-story, columned, white clapboard home is set in the middle of the block and is surrounded by tall, spreading trees. Towering Crow Mountain overlooks the Inn to the north, and the old house still retains the regal bearing it did many years ago as the first big house in the area.

Pennsylvania native Kirkbride Potts originally came to Arkansas in 1828 to homestead. He married Pamelia Allison Logan of Logan County and, in the early 1840's, purchased from the U.S. Government 160 acres of land in Pope County on Galla Creek. The Potts had eleven children and, after outgrowing their log house, decided to build a 'dream' home. Construction began in 1850 and, finally in 1858, Posts was financially able to complete his impressive house.

The combination home and Inn was sturdily constructed, with slaves doing most of the work. Area timber was used for the hand-cut lumber, and bricks were all hand molded by slaves. The frame of the house was fitted with mortise joints and held securely with wooden pegs. The fireplace mantels were brought up the Arkansas River by boat, as were the windows and glass panes, many of which are still in the house today.

In the big yard surrounding the home, 13 buildings were raised, including a stagecoach house, saddle house and slave cabins. The smokehouse and well house still stand beneath the massive branches of an old bois d'arc tree, and future restoration plans call for reproductions of the other outbuildings...

Continuing up rock steps to a two-story portico, entrance to the Inn is through two double doors. Once inside, visitors will find themselves in a 12 foot wide hallway. It was here that local residents once came to pick up their mail.

Opening off the Inn's large hallway are four spacious rooms, all 20 feet square and each containing a fireplace. One of the front rooms is known as the public room and formerly served as a lounging and meeting area for governors, military officers, Indian chiefs, lawyers and the socially prominent when Potts Inn was a 'house of public entertainment.'

...Opposite the public room is the Potts' parlor where all of the daughters and granddaughters in the family were married. It is adjoined by a guest bedroom that provided comfortable lodging to countless dignitaries. Across the hall is a large dining room, where guest dined with the Potts at a long table...

Upstairs, the Potts' home is arranged and sized exactly like the first floor. Four large bedrooms with fireplaces and wall-to-wall beds provided amble room for family and their guests, and a huge attic above was often used for sleeping quarters when the Inn had an overflow.

On the back of the Inn, connected by a breezeway and porch, is the Potts kitchen, 17 by 20 feet, with a massive fireplace once used for cooking."

Next to the kitchen fireplace at Potts Station there was a bath tub available to overnight passengers who wished to buy a bath.
Photo by Bob Crossman, 2024

POTTS INN

Kirkbride Potts, with help from his wife Pamelia Logan Potts, designed and constructed this large and stately building between 1850 and 1858. He patterned it after the Classical Revival style he knew in his home state of Pennsylvania; however, he built it with local labor and native materials. Lumber for siding and trim, bricks for chimneys, and laths and plaster for walls were designed and finished on site. Only doors, mantels, and glass window panes were factory made and shipped up the Arkansas River.

The building served as a post office, a social and cultural center, an inn, overnight Butterfield Stage stop, and home. The Butterfield line closed at the beginning of the War in 1861. With the stage line gone and four years of devastating war and its aftermath, Potts Inn changed. The inn provided fine accommodations for early travelers and new customers. For example, it furnished food and lodging for surveyors and engineers working for the Little Rock and Fort Smith Railway Company.

Pamelia Potts died August 5, 1878 and Kirkbride followed, November 27, 1879. Both are buried in Potts Cemetery overlooking the land of Galla Creek. Potts' descendants occupied the home until they sold it to the Pope County Historical Foundation in 1970.

NATIONAL REGISTER OF HISTORICAL PLACES
1970

John Kirkbride Potts (1803–1879)

His story is best told in the Encyclopedia of Arkansas:

"John Kirkbride Potts laid the groundwork for the founding of the town of Pottsville (Pope County). He patented 160 acres of land between Crow Mountain and the Arkansas River and later enlarged his holdings to 650 acres. His house, which served as a post office and railroad rest stop, was entered in the National Register of Historic Places on June 22, 1970, and is now a museum.

John Kirkbride Potts was born in Pennsylvania on March 24, 1803, to Joshua Potts and Mary (Bunting) Potts. He had five siblings. The family moved from Pennsylvania to New Jersey in 1812.

At age seventeen, Potts went west, traveling by wagon with two slave families to Wayne County, Missouri, where he met William Logan and Robert A. Logan. They traveled to and settled in an area in the Arkansas River bottom, south of Mount Magazine. When the 1828 federal treaty removed the Cherokee and white settlers, both groups were granted preemptive privileges entailing safe passage and land patents.

Potts and the Logans moved southeast across the Arkansas River to Galla Rock (Pope County), a river port. Potts had served as an agent for the Bureau of Indian Affairs during the removal of Cherokee and Choctaw to the Cherokee Nation.

Potts married Robert Logan's daughter Pamelia on February 10, 1829. The couple eventually had eleven children, nine living to adulthood.

In 1828, Potts had exercised his preemptive privilege from being removed by using his land patents to buy from the government, making it possible for him to buy his first 160 acres for twenty-five cents an acre. A land patent is nothing more than a document attesting to the right of own-

ership to a tract of land granted by a state or the federal government to an individual or company. Through various additional patents, he enlarged his land holdings to 650 acres. He chose a high spot at the foot of Crow Mountain near Galla Creek and built a two-level log house for his growing family and lived there for twenty-five years.

We do not have a photo of Kirkbride Potts' 1828 two story log house. Most likely it was similar to this ca. 1834 home in northwest Arkansas.
Photo: John Latta residence on the grounds of the Prairie Grove Battlefield State Park.
Image in Public Domain

"After hearing news of the gold rush, Potts and others in the community went to California in 1849. He failed to strike gold but found that the miners would pay well for cattle. He made at least two cattle drives in 1850's, staying long enough to graze and fatten the cattle and eventually profiting enough to return to Arkansas and build a much grander home on a hill south of the family's first log house.

Kirkbride had apparently been thinking about a grander house for years, based on a letter to his sister in Pennsylvania a decade earlier asking her about house plan ideas.

"Nov. 3, 1848: Could you get the draft of a convenient farm house and send it to me? I told you I had an idea of building and I am at a loss for a good and convenient plan to build upon. We have had a great deal of company since we got home and being in such a public place we have not house room enough. Last night, we had 13 members with us going to the Legislature and we have someone almost every night."

There is a legend that in 1849, upon returning from his California gold prospecting trip, Kirkbride stopped by the Little Rock newspaper editor's office and gave him a gold nugget.

After making note of high cattle prices in California, Potts returned to the west driving a herd of cattle for market. Potts made a third trip to California on April 22, 1856, with a second herd of 300+ head of cattle. He had purchased them in Arkansas for $5 a head and anticipated selling them in California for about 13¢ a pound on the hoof. These three California trips provided funds to complete construction of a grand home for his 11 children.

All the brick was molded, and the timber was cut by enslaved labor. They hauled the timber by oxen to Cagle's Mill, north of Norristown, to be sawed into lumber. The lumber was dressed by hand, with beams affixed with mortise joints and wood pegs as still visible in the ample attic. The two story home has four 17' x 20' rooms on each floor, two on each side of a central hallway. The construction, by enslaved workers living on the Potts property, lasted six years. The quality of the construction is evident in that the home it still standing today, 166 years later.

Descendants remember that there were about fourteen outbuildings, including: barns for stagecoach horses, chicken house, leather tack house, carriage house for Potts wagons, smoke house, well house, two houses for enslaved workers, and two outhouses - a 5 hole and a 2 hole.

(Sources: Kirkbride Potts' letter from Red Bluffs, California to the editor of the Arkansas Gazette, published July 25, 1857, page 2; from an article in the Russellville Courier Democrat, April 17, 1994 'The House That Potts Built'; and a site plan drawn by great grandson.)

The house's completion in 1858 coincided with John Butterfield's organization of the Overland Mail Company and his 1857 procurement of a contract to carry mail from St. Louis and Memphis to Fort Smith (Sebastian County), then west to San Francisco. The route from Memphis went by Potts's new home, which became a comfortable rest stop. Because of its two and a half stories, many fireplaces, and large detached kitchens, many prominent people stopped at the house for social events or while traveling.

The house became known as Potts Station and was a center for shipping and mail. Potts was appointed postmaster by the president of the United States. Mail was handled in the living room using a desk that Potts had designed and built.

Potts Station in the Snow
Photo by Allan Motley, 2021

The house became a hotel, called Potts Inn, after the stagecoach stopped; however, it was still widely known as Potts Station until the town that grew up around it became Pottsville. The Potts family sold the house to the Pope County Historical Foundation in 1970, and it is now a museum for the Pope County Historical Foundation. It is listed on the National Register of Historic Places.

Having never fully recovered from the death of his wife in August 1878, Potts died on November 24, 1879, in Potts Station from a severe form of dyspepsia [abdominal pain, nausea and indigestion], and he was buried in the Potts Cemetery near the center of the town.

"Kirkbride Potts," Encyclopedia of Arkansas
https://encyclopediaofarkansas.net/entries/john-kirkbride-potts-78

Twenty years after Kirkbride's death, in 1897, Pottsville was incorporated with the name of "Pottsville" at the suggestion of James Potts in honor of his father.

Potts Inn, ca. 1970
View of the south side of the home showing the two chimneys. Originally all the chimneys were made of brick. One of the chimney crumpled in 1910 and was replaced using native rock. (Russellville Courier Democrat, April 17, 1994 'The House That Potts Built') Image compliments of Margaret Motley

Historical Marker on Potts Inn Chimney
*The marker was placed on northeast chimney during the 1958 Butterfield Centennial celebration.
Image compliments of Margaret Motley*

Potts Station Site Plan for Entire Block

A great-grandson of Kirkbride and Pamelia Potts, James Allison Johnson, drew this site plan of the Potts Station block as he remembered it from the 1930's. James spent time as a child with this grandparents, James and Ada Potts at the Inn.

Source: "The Potts Family and Early Pottsville" by Margaret Motley and Kara Bowers, 2022, page 15.

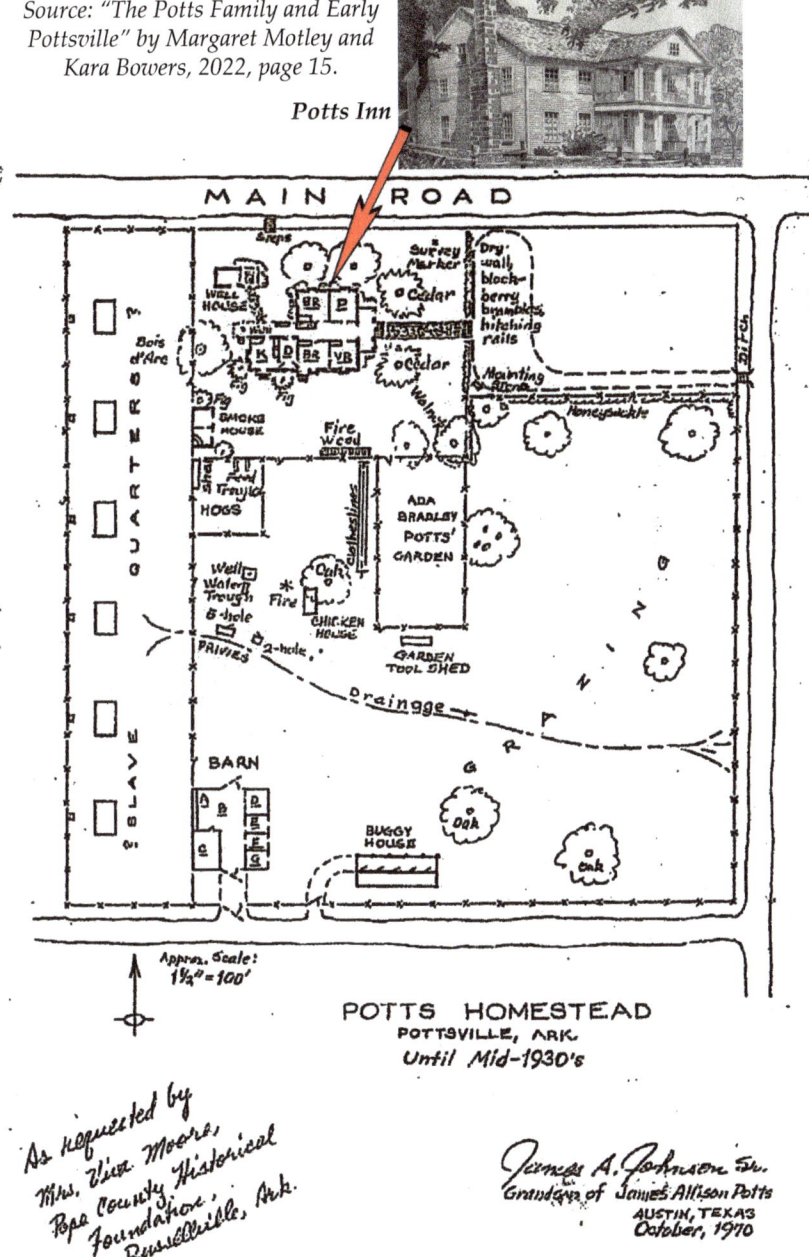

Potts Inn - A Place to Hold Grand Events

The 1882 wedding reception at Potts Inn was a grand event similar to this 1874 wedding event illustration reproduced in Frank Leslie's Newspaper.

November 2, 1882

"Unquestionably the most charming social event of the season was the soiree at the Pott's Mansion, Galla Creek Station, on last Tuesday evening, the affair assuming the phase of an impromptu reception in honor of the newly wedded couple, Mr. Jeff Davis and bride, nee Ina McKenzie of Russellville.

First of all, the evening was scarcely short of what we might imagine an evening in Fairy-land-to-be — bright with the silvery moonbeams from full-faced Luna, smiling from her orb on high, balmy with the rich and mellow autumnal air; fresh and bracing in the purity of an atmosphere clear, and soft, and bright; and lastly musical and resonant with the ringing laughter of many merry couples as they gleefully chatted and laughed and sang on their way over the six-mile drive from the town of Galla Creek.

The road was just in its best plight and as the gay party sped lightly over the smooth prairie, even the hills and mountains which gird the prairie round about, like margin closing in some placid lake, seemed to clap their hands and nod their heads in salutation to the merry cavalcade as they dashed along.

The Potts' mansion has long been known far and wide as the home of hospitality and good cheer; and as the marry-makers drew near, the brightly illuminated halls and parlors threw out a light from many a door and window, inviting in, with outstretched arms, the evening's guests.

Once within the spacious parlor jest and repartee and gayety and laughter ruled the hour. Surely the most gallant beaux and charming belles in the land were there, and without the slightest thing to mar the mirthful measure of time's flight all went as merry as a marriage bell until ten o'clock, when with a kind of fairy enchantment-like change, the music and card tables gave way for the rarest cakes and lemonades, and the estimable hostess invited all to a repast as rare and elegant as the occasion itself.

'Twas 12 o'clock, or near, when the merry throng began to make their leave. To the attentive hostess of the evening, Mr. R. B. Potts, assisted by Mr. Jamison and Mrs. Davis, the guests, each and all, fell under a debt of gratitude for the splendid time they had enjoyed."

This 1892 reception at Potts Inn was in honor of the marriage of Jeff Davis and Ina McKenzie of Russellville. Jeff Davis would later become the Governor of Arkansas. *Source: "The Potts Family and Early Pottsville" by Margaret Motley and Kara Bowers, 2022, page 135-136.*

Trail of Tears in Arkansas

Trail of Tears Map

Image compliments of the Northwest Arkansas Democrat & Gazette, March 25, 2014

The Trail of Tears passed by the Kirkbride Potts log cabin home he built in 1828.

The travel of a group of Creeks in the 1836 forced removal is recorded in Capt. F. S. Belton's *"Journal of Occurrences - Indian Removal of Creeks,"* he writes:

17 September 1836

Left Mathers and passed Point Remove creek by Fletchers toll bridge. The bottom is probably the worst on the road and nearly impassable. Halted at Blounts old place 4 miles beyond Point Remove. 12 miles.

18 September, 1836.

The party reached Potts. Road very bad and rain in heavy torrents. 12 miles - The condition of the wagons here requires a days work at the blacksmith shop. Distance 12 miles.

19 September 1836.

A teamster is taken violently ill. Place supplied by Indian Ben as he must be left. The conductor and agent is also taken sick. Met Lt Barry on his return from Fort Gibson.

20 September 1836.

Rain-Party moved early reached Lovely's place. Passed Illinois Bayou by ferry below old Dwight. Rain in drenching torrents and waters very high and rapid.

This was not the only group that camped at Kirkbride Potts two-story log cabin.

There was also a group of 2,000 Creeks and their 500 ponies that left Tallahassee, Florida on Sept.5, 1836. Reaching Little Rock on Nov. 4, 1836, they followed what would later be called THE BUTTERFIELD NATIONAL HISTORIC TRAIL westward to Indian Territory.

About mid Nov. 1836, the report reads, *"Camp at Potts near Lewisburg. Arrive at Kirkbride Potts at Pottsville. Camp near the river Spadra* (near Clarksville) ...*Nov. 24, 1836."*

Chief Tuck-a-batch-i-had-jo & Potts Log Cabin

Ken Harper, Margaret Motley and Kara Bowers shared this great story with me. It is a story found in the *Arkansas Historical Quarterly,* that reports the movements of the Cherokee Indians through Pope County to Port Gibson for settlement in the Oklahoma Territory in the 1830's. The story goes like this:

"In the midst of forced relocation from the Atlantic states to Indian Territory *(Oklahoma), ...Chief Tuck-a-batch-i-had-jo* stopped just above Potts place in Pope County and declared that he would go no farther. The chief had interpreted the terms of the treaty with the federal government to mean that his people were to move west of the Mississippi, and clearly-by the time the Potts place was reached – they were west of the Mississippi. The chief had been threatened with force if he did not move on, but he ridiculed the idea.

A month after *Chief Tuck-a-batch-i-had-jo* was first reported to be a few miles west of Potts, he was still refusing to budge. Kirkbride Potts, the owner of the plantation referred to above, probably believed that the proximity of the Indians was a nuisance though nothing specific is mentioned to indicate that his unwelcome neighbors had molested him. Anyway, about Christmas of 1836, Potts went over to the Indian encampment *(alone as far as the record is concerned)* and asked the Indians to be on their way. The chief repeated what he had said before, that he was west of the Mississippi and would go no farther, the chief contended,

'They said that the threat of the whites might alarm little boys — but they were men!' It appears that Potts then notified Colonel Trevault, commandant of the Pope County militia, that the Indians were stubborn. *'In two or three days upwards of 100 mounted men appeared, for a forcible expulsion. But they were not needed — the Indians getting wind of the movement, decamped in the night about the first of January, and made a precipitate flight.'* [Arkansas Historical Quarterly, Vol. 6, pages 161-162]

In the Dec. 16, 1836, *Arkansas Advocate,* we read: *'Tuck-a-batch-i-had-jo has stopped just above Potts, and declares he will go no farther. He says he is west of the Mississippi, and can be compelled to go no farther — and when threatened that force would be used to make him remove, he has ridiculed the idea.'* " [Arkansas Advocate, Dec. 16, 1836, p.1]

Local Legend About Gold & 1858 Potts Inn

In 1858, Seminole Chief Bowlegs and 123 of his tribe agreed to relocate to Indian Territory *(Oklahoma)*.

They agreed to relocate when the U.S. government paid Bowlegs $10,000 in gold, each of his chiefs $1,000, and a smaller amount to each warrior.

In May of 1858, this group left Florida on the steam ship *Grey Cloud,* and arrived in New Orleans. On May 19, 1858 Bowlegs and his tribe boarded the steamboat *Qua-*

Chief Bowlegs
Published by Rice, Rutter & Co., 20 x 12 9/16 in 1872-1874

paw, and steamed up the Mississippi and the Arkansas Rivers toward Indian Territory. *[The Time-Picayune, May 19, 1858, p.3]* The *Quapaw*, under command of Captain Danley, arrived in Little Rock on May 25, 1858, and departed toward Fort Smith that same day. *[Weekly Arkansas Gazette, May 29, 1858, p.3]*

The Steamboat, Quapaw

The *Arkansas Gazette* reported: "Billy Bowlegs – This distinguished Indian passed up [the river], *on the steamboat Quapaw, en route for his new home west of this State. While we have a great contempt for the small material out of which Indian heroes (and white ones too) are generally manufactured, we think Billy will be written down by future impartial historians of our country, as a man of mark.*

Billy Bowlegs, with the merest handful of men, and encumbered with their women and children, for more than twenty years, successfully defied the whole military power of the United States. And, at last, he was not captured by force, but emigrated peacefully – the government giving himself and his people **a large sum of money***, and a country west of this State for a home in future. The Seminole war, and its heroes, will furnish ample material for future writers of both history and fiction."* [*Weekly Arkansas Gazette, May 29, 1858, p.2*]

A local legend about Indians and kegs of gold may be referring to Chief Bowlegs' 1st or 2nd trip up the Arkansas River. Perhaps it was on his first trip, that Chief deboarded the *Quapaw* with several of his braves, and traveled up Gally Creek to spend the night near Potts Inn before continuing west on the *Quapaw*.

James Potts told his granddaughter Mary, that late one afternoon his father, Kirkbride Potts was sitting on the veranda when a wagon train and horsemen appeared. He noted that one wagon was guarded by a man on the seat with the driver, who had a rifle on his lap and a horseman on either side with a rifle across his saddle. A dignified Seminole [Was this Chief Billy Bowlegs?] alighted and asked permission to camp on the premises. Permission was granted. He then asked permission to place some kegs on the porch for the night. This permission was also granted and kegs were lined up on the porch like watermelons.

James Potts, 11 years of age at the time, and some of the little enslaved boys found it great sport to ride atop these kegs on the porch, as small boys will. James later learned that the kegs were filled with gold coins which had been paid to the Seminole for their lands in their old home in Florida.

From another source we find James was told by his father that these Indians camped on the small hill where the Pottsville Fire Station is located today. [Memories of My Early Years," Mary Johnson Hawkins Hall, 2003, page 58]

If this was Chief Billy Bowlegs, the next morning he must have collected his kegs of gold off the Potts Inn porch, reboarded the *Quapaw* to arrive in Van Buren May 27, 1858, entering Indian Territory June 10, 1858.

The next day, the Van Buren newspaper reported, *"Major Rector, Superintendent of Indian Affairs on this frontier, arrived on Thursday night last, on the steamer Quapaw, having in charge the renowned Seminole chief, Billy Bowlegs, and about one hundred other Florida Indians, en route for the Seminole nation. Another delegation of the same tribe arrived this morning on the steamer Arkansaw."* [Arkansas Intelligencer, May 28, 1858]

On June 11th, newspapers reported: *"Billy Bowlegs and the rest of the Seminoles have departed for their new home."* [Arkansas Intelligencer, June 11, 1858, p.2]

The Quapaw was apparently paid $3,500 for making the trip. [True Democrat, June, 1858 p.2]

Potts Inn During the Civil War

Colonel Samuel A. Rice
of 33rd Iowa Infantry

HISTORY

OF THE

33D IOWA INFANTRY

VOLUNTEER REGIMENT

1863-6

BY A. F. SPERRY

During the Civil War, the 33rd Iowa Union troops, briefly stopped at the Potts 1858 Tavern, in 1864. The *"History of the 33rd Iowa Infantry"* records the visit:

"*On the night of November 5, 1864, we camped some eleven miles west of Lewisburg... During this halt dispatches were received, announcing the defeat of Price and his rebels in Missouri, and their scattered retreat toward the Arkansas river.*

On the 7th, starting on again, we make about fourteen miles, and camped for the night around the residence of a Mr. Potts, an arrant old rebel.

A large white house, with big barns and granaries, commanding a near view of the abrupt and imposing 'Carrion-Crow Mountain,' it would have been a good enough home for a much better man.

Foraging was prohibited, but not prevented, and the secesh proprietor of the premises unwillingly contributed to the Union army enough to make us two pretty good meals, at least, and very probably suffered the loss of more.

*All along the road, the country hereabouts seemed to be good, and well settled. The women and children appeared to be all gathered at the neighbors' houses to look at us, while the men were out in the woods 'bushwhacking.' There was *considerable apprehension among us of trouble with these bushwhackers, and frequent reports came of our having been fired upon from the sides of the road; but most or all of these stories, when traced up, were found to start from some wagon-master or train-teamster.*

About 1:30 P. M., of November 8th, we camped in a field on the Illinois bayou, three miles from Russellville...

That night it rained hard, and did not stop till it turned cold the next morning. This made a very uncomfortable time. A warm rain, if followed by a clear, warm day, is little heeded in the army; but a soaking flood of water, followed only by clouds, cold and winds, is exceedingly unwelcome. Resuming the march, we found that the bayou, had risen several inches; and as there was no other means of crossing, we had to wade through it. The cold, raw wind, as well as the coldness of the water, spoiled all the fun of the thing..."

Source: History of the 33rd Iowa, pages 109-110

**Battle Flag of the 33rd Iowa
Infantry Volunteer Regiment**

Wagon Trail to Galla Rock?
NW¼ of SE¼, Section 29, 7N 19W

On July 1, 2024, Dr. Daniel Littlefield Jr. from the University of Arkansas, along with Margaret Motley, Kara Bowers, Bob Crossman, and local land owner Eric Edens, explored the remnants of an old wagon trail two miles due south of Potts Inn along Galla Creek. This trail on Eric Edens land appears to be the old trail between Potts Station and the steamboat landing at Galla Rock on the Arkansas River.

Eric Edens, Bob Crossman and Daniel Littlefield examining an 1850 survey map of this section.

This old wagon trail runs due north and south on the property of Eric Edens. It appears to be the wagon trail connecting the Butterfield Trail and Potts Station with the steamboat landing at Galla Rock on the Arkansas River. This trail would have been used a great deal between 1828-1872, before the railroad began to replace the steamboat as the primary means of transportation.

Kara Bowers, Margaret Motley, Dr. Daniel Littlefield, and Eric Edens on the July 1, 2024 inspection of the old trail.

Search for Kirkbride's 1828 Log Cabin Site

In 1828, Kirkbride Potts built a two story log cabin near the location of today's Pottsville, Arkansas.

Descendant David Potts, was told that in 1828 Kirkbride built a two story log cabin on a high spot at the foot of Crow Mountain near Galla Creek, and that thirty years later, in 1858, Kirkbride built the present "Potts Inn" ½ mile south of that log cabin.

The Potts family tradition locates the original log cabin within the green box below - this 160 acre parcel is between I40 and the foot of Crow Mountain.

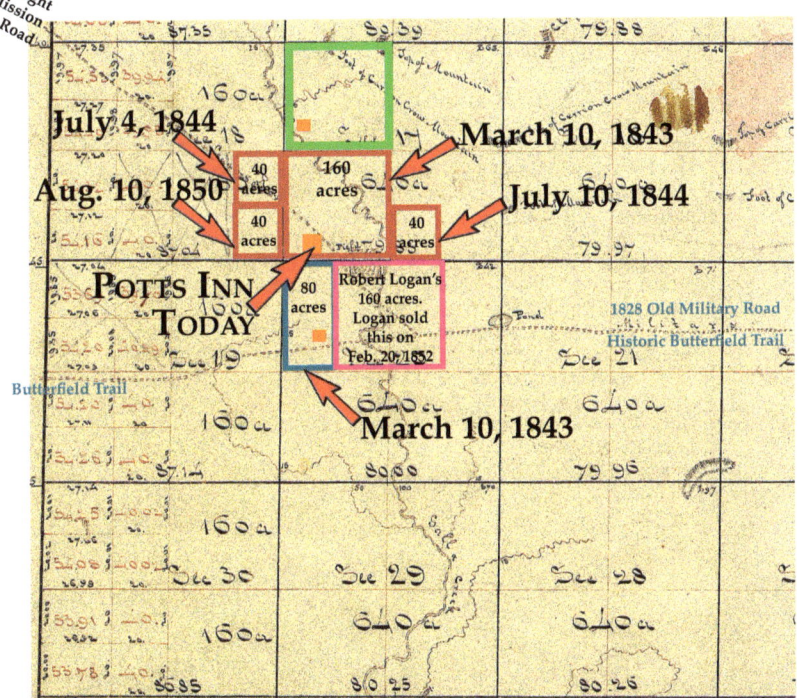

This map shows the date Kirkbride recorded his purchase of various parcels near his 1858 home that is still standing.

Bob Crossman speculates that Kirkbride's 1828 log cabin was on the 80 acres *(blue box)* along the 1828 Military road, based on Kirkbride's July 1, 1830 letter: *"living here on a public road where... two hundred families moved by us last fall... Robert Logan lives ½ mile from me..."* Research is still seeking Kirkbride's original 1828 land documents.

Kirkbride Potts died on November 24, 1879

DEATH OF KIRKBRIDE POTTS

We are permitted, by a friend, to copy the following telegram, dated Russellville, November 25th:

My father passed away without the least expression of suffering, at 9:30 o'clock last night.   JAMES POTTS.

Thus another of the old pioneers has been gathered to his fathers. He had reached the allotted period of man's existence, and died surrounded by his large family of grown and married children. In the full possession of his mental faculties and without pain, as the dispatch says, he passed away. He died at the old homestead, which is now known as Potts' station, on the Fort Smith railroad, where, more than half a century ago, with his iron will and strong arm he had invaded the solitude of nature, and where, by the efforts of a long and industrious life, he had surrounded himself with more than an ordinary share of this world's goods. He sent three stalwart sons to follow the fortunes of the confederate flag, and received only two of them back again. Arkansas never had a better citizen than Kirkbride Potts, and his many friends who cherish the memory of his useful and honorable life will feel a pang of genuine sorrow when they learn that he is no more.

The hilltop Potts Family Cemetery
The Potts family cemetery is a short walk northeast from the Potts Tavern, on the north side of the railroad tracks.

The Pottsville United Methodist Church

In 1847, a Methodist Episcopal South Church started in Pottsville. In 1873, they shared their first building with the Masonic Lodge. In 1924 they moved to their present site.

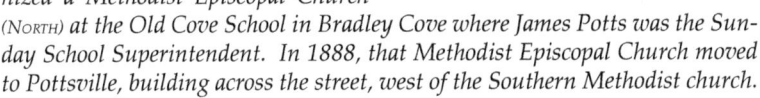

In 1868, Rev. L. C. O'Barr organized a Methodist Episcopal Church (NORTH) at the Old Cove School in Bradley Cove where James Potts was the Sunday School Superintendent. In 1888, that Methodist Episcopal Church moved to Pottsville, building across the street, west of the Southern Methodist church. In 1939, these two Methodist congregations merged together.

The author, Bob Crossman, was the pastor of this congregation from March 1978 until June 1980. At that time he had the good fortune to be the pastor for the family of George and Helen Potts.

Sketch of Potts Tavern by Joe Gray, 1976

Traveling West of Potts Inn

Norristown Station west of Potts Inn

Departing the Potts Inn station, the stage traveled nine miles west to the Norristown station, then crossed the ferry to Dardanelle and continued westward toward Fort Smith.

Discovery of the Norristown Station & the Dardanelle Ferry
N 35.238635, W -93.158547

The Butterfield Overland Mail Co. used the 1828 Old Military Road traveling on the north side of the Arkansas River between Argenta (North Little Rock) and the ferry at Norristown to avoid the barriers of Petit Jean Mountain and the bayous at Petit Jean, Fourche LeFevre, and Maumelle.

Old Norristown Stage Station

Mike Goad reports that *"in the early 1800's, the Illinois Bayou was a meandering stream instead of what we see today. Dwight Mission was a missionary settlement along the bayou's bank. Part of its actual site may now be below Dardanelle Lake. Indian Agent William Lovely's widow, Persis, at the request of the Cherokee, was to be allowed, in an 1817 treaty 'to remain for life' at her home next to the agency. In the May 6, 1828, Treaty with The Western Cherokee that relinquished the Arkansas lands of the Cherokee, that provision was missing. In an 1830 letter, she wrote, 'In consequence I am a houseless wanderer at sixty years of age.' Norristown was on the river and, during the 1830s, would see displaced thousands crossing on the Norristown ferry to follow the military road laid out by Lieutenant Jefferson Davis to the Indian Territory."* Source: Mike Goad, *"Remember Russellville, Then & Now"*

The Norristown stage stop is mentioned in the 1919 Charles T. Davis article in the Gazette, *"The Town That Disappeared"* he writes:

"On the Pope county bank of the Arkansas, a little north of and diagonally across the river from Dardanelle Rock on the Yell county side, stands a little, weather-warped, time-shaken log house but of a single room and a native stone chimney out of all proportion to its size.

This little cabin is all that remains of Norristown, one time the most important town between Fort Smith and Little Rock on the north side of the river... **At one time it was a commodious two-story tavern known widely throughout the state. It was there that the creaking stage coaches drew up from the South and East** *...nothing remains but a shadow of the old post road along which the splendid relay teams once plunged with the mails from the East to the West—now but a little, weed-grown country lane maintained simply to give a few farmers entrance to their fields...*

> According to Charles T. Davis, this one room log cabin, formerly Cephas Washburn's home, was the Butterfield Station at Norristown. Below, Davis also refers to a 2nd "change station" across the river at Dardanelle.

While Norristown was one of the most important points on the post road between Little Rock and Fort Smith, Dardanelle, **just across the river, was the** *'change' station.* **The mail or the 'post' was carried overland in stage coaches, drawn by four horses,** *and as near as can now be gathered there were four relays. Out of Little Rock teams were changed at what is now Gleason in Faulkner county, at Lewisburg in Conway county, at Dardanelle in what is now Yell county, at what is now Paris, or thereabout, in Logan county, and so into Fort Smith.* **At Norristown, the stage crossed the river on Tate's ferry.**

...The stage coach was a cumbersome affair slung without springs on leather straps from arches up — ending at the axles. The bump of the road was relieved only by the forward and back swaying of the body suspended from the straps, and the mail and baggage were carried in the 'boot,' a small platform swung at the rear. The horses were magnificent animals, the best obtainable and the drivers were widely known over their 'runs.' ..there was adequate ferriage across the river at Norristown for lighter traffic, such as the stage coaches and private conveyances..."

Old log home of Cephas Washburn at Norristown, Arkansas
In 1855, Cephas Washburn, founder of Dwight Presbyterian Mission on Illinois Bayou west of present-day Russellville, moved to Norristown where he worked as a minister and was instrumental in the establishment of Presbyterian churches at Dardanelle and Galley (Galla) Rock. **[According to Charles T. Davis, this was the Butterfield Station at Norristown.]**

Dwight Mission near Norristown, Arkansas
In 1820 Cephas Washburn founded the Dwight Cherokee Mission, the first school in Arkansas. When Cherokees were removed from the area in 1828, the school also relocated to Indian Territory. Daguerreotype, ca 1842-1856.

1866 Letter to the Editor From Norristown

Weekly Arkansas Gazette, Little Rock, Arkansas, Tue, Dec 18, 1866, Page 2

Dear Gazette,   December, 1866

...Norristown... it is situate in a crook of the Arkansas valley, the finest, by the way, in all the known world. I live in the 'outsquirts' of this town...

Norristown is certainly a town though some might call it a hamlet... It is a place celebrated muchly for many things...

It is celebrated for being the finest site on the river betwixt Fort Smith and Little Rock, which, the owners thereof seduously seclude from the world by asking fabulous prices for lots.

It is a most extraordinarily healthy place — no man ever having been known to die here, unless he was shot in the war.

It was settled about the year of Grace, 1818, by one Walter Webber, a Cherokee Chief, a warrior of renown, and a merchant who sold his $50,000 per year, and took his pay in bear, deer and panther skins, pecans and gold...

It has got the oldest apple tree in the State, a huge, crooked, ugly, gnarled, crabbed, worthless tree, whose trunk would furnish the finest stock in the world to a "Greener" shot-gun... The Lord only knows how many urchins have eaten of its fruit, and how terrible were the stomach aches consequent...

Theres not a lawyer, nor a doctor in the place.

Too moral for the one, too healthy for the other.

There's is no preacher here either; everybody reads his Bible and follows its precepts, so none is needed. There is one school... Not a grocery nor saloon. Of course it is a temperate place...

Once in a while a beef is butchered here. The event is barometrical. You can tell the temperament of the citizens by it. A few hours after the bovine luxury gets in, everybody's face is smiling with good humor. We all meet and crack our jokes, for we have all had meat. But, alas, beef don't come in every day. We get hungry. We wear long faces; we get sour and sometimes cross. We go about peeping through the cracks of smoke houses, smelling if anybody is got any meat. Beef! Beef! Beef!

...There is a transient smithy here...

There is also a town well... It is a mighty wild well and needs curbing.

There is one store here, Perry & Tobey.

They have also as fine a horse power cotton gin as there is in the state.

A mill is also here... most excellent flour you can get there... Only two faults to this mill: one, there's not enough wheat to grind, and the other, that, therefore the proprietor is compelled to charge high for what he grinds...

No Post Office here... a neighboring postmaster contrives to get here once in a while — angelic visits — the citizens hereof would forget that they lived in the United States.

Norristown is also famous for another thing, a botanic celebrity, and that is, the Truett red round turnip. They are fine, luscious, succulent, and the fat pigs root around the patch, squealing to be cooked with so excellent a vegetable. I walked into said patch, the other day... I selected one at random for measure. It circled twenty-one inches. That's what I call a turnip. The Squire ought to send you a bushel.

But the crowning glory of the town is the Dardanelles Rock. It is a 'thing of beauty and a joy forever.' It lifts its scarred, jarred, tinted and rifted face everlastingly before the town, eternal, changeless and beautiful. I never tire of studying that face of carboniferous sand stone Trappe. Some mornings, just as the sun gilds the west, the tints of the particolored oxydes on its face grow marvelously beautiful in the kissing light of the new day' and the full splendor of a full moon — it is absolutely glorious; while in the chill, bleak and forty days of cold and cloud, it reminds me of the gray face and head of an Apollo in his time of three score and ten. What histories has that rock of myriads of ages stored; and how far, far, far back in the achingly long tramp of time does it carry me as I look upon its summit, so calm for thousands of centuries after that convulsion which upheaved it!

Mr. Editor, this is getting to be a tiresomely long scrawl, isn't it?

...Pope County is a quiet as a lamb...

Here's a glass of nog to you, this [December] 25th...

Yours, J. W. W.

Norristown is also Famous for "The Arkansas Traveler"

The son of the early Norristown settler, Cephas Washburn, is the artist who painted "The Arkansas Traveler." In 1858 Edward Payson Washburn, resident of Norristown, painted what became the trademark image of the State of Arkansas.

The Ferry at Dardanelle

When the Overland Mail reached Norristown, nine miles west of Potts Inn, they continued to follow the 1828 Old Military Road, crossing the Arkansas River by ferry to Dardanelle, then continuing toward Fort Smith on the south side of the Arkansas River. *[Arkansas Gazette, Jan. 3, 1826, page 3]*

In 1872, upon the occasion of a circus crossing the river, the Dardanelle ferry was described in the newspaper: *"The ferry was simply a flat-boat arrangement, and of course necessarily slow and tedious.."* [Little Rock Republican, Nov. 5, 1872]

More than likely, based on the newspaper description above, the Dardanelle ferry at the time of Butterfield's Overland looked something like this flat boat ferry pictured below that was on the Missouri River in Kansas.

We do not have a photo of the Dardanelle flat-boat ferry from 1858. Most likely is was similar to this "Flatboat Crossing the Missouri River"ca.1870 Cowley County Historical Society Museum, Winfield, Kansas

Jacob Shinn

Jacob L. Shinn bought and owned the Dardanelle Ferry. It was said to be one of the best boats to ever float on the Arkansas River. At one time he owned nearly 2,000 acres of land. *["Russellville Centennial 1870-1970"]*

Jacob L. Shinn

Location of the Dardanelle Ferry Site

The location of the ferry site is known from the following 1827 and 1877 maps in the Arkansas State Archives.

Butterfield Overland National Historic Trail Through Arkansas' Pope & Conway Counties

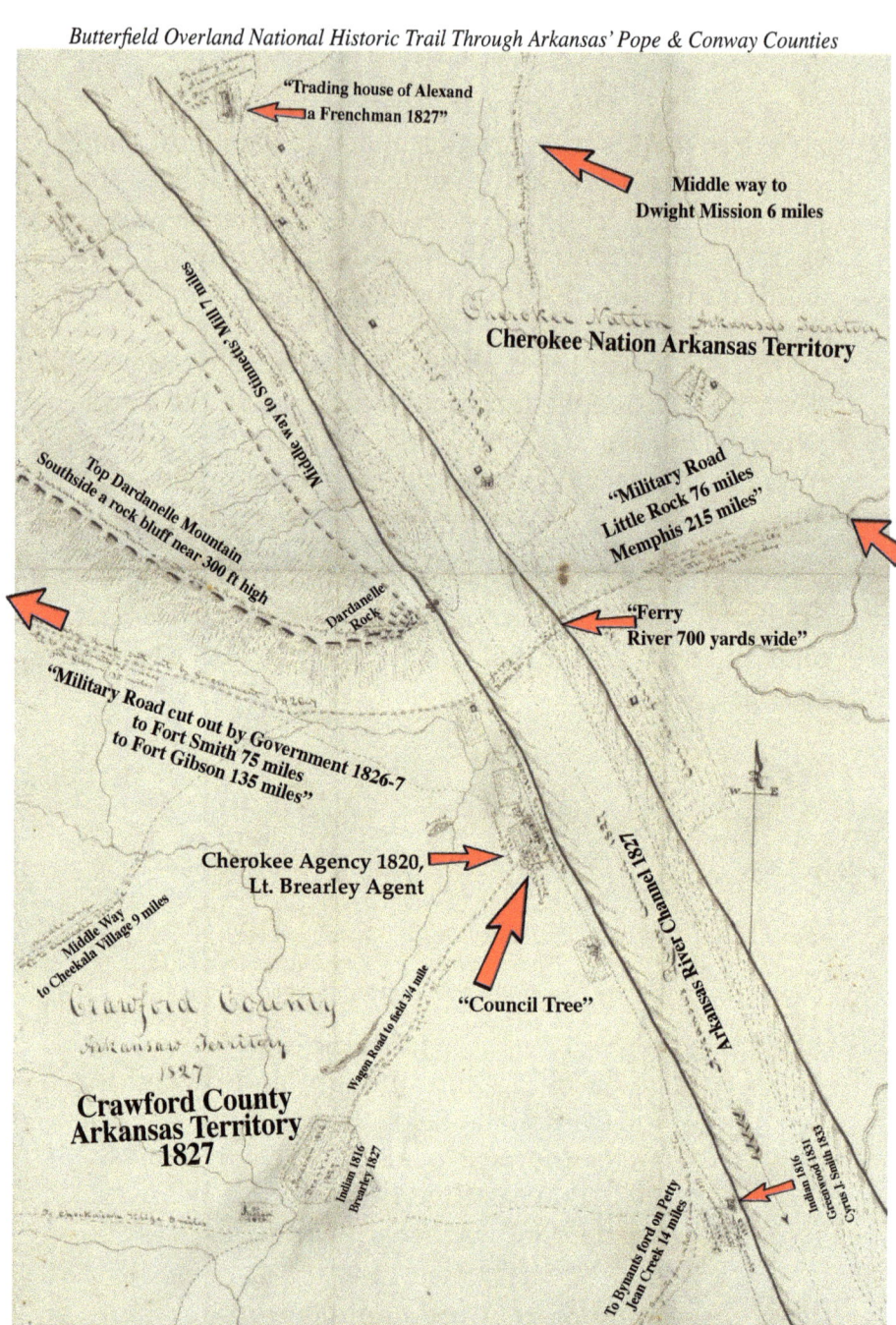

1827 Arkansas Territory Map Showing Indian Agent's home and ferry crossing
*Also shows the 1826 Military Road that connects Fort Smith and Little Rock.
Council Tree is where the Territorial Governor met with the Cherokee chief in 1823.
Map 0194, Map collection inventory, Arkansas State Archives, Little Rock, AR*

Butterfield Overland National Historic Trail Through Arkansas' Pope & Conway Counties

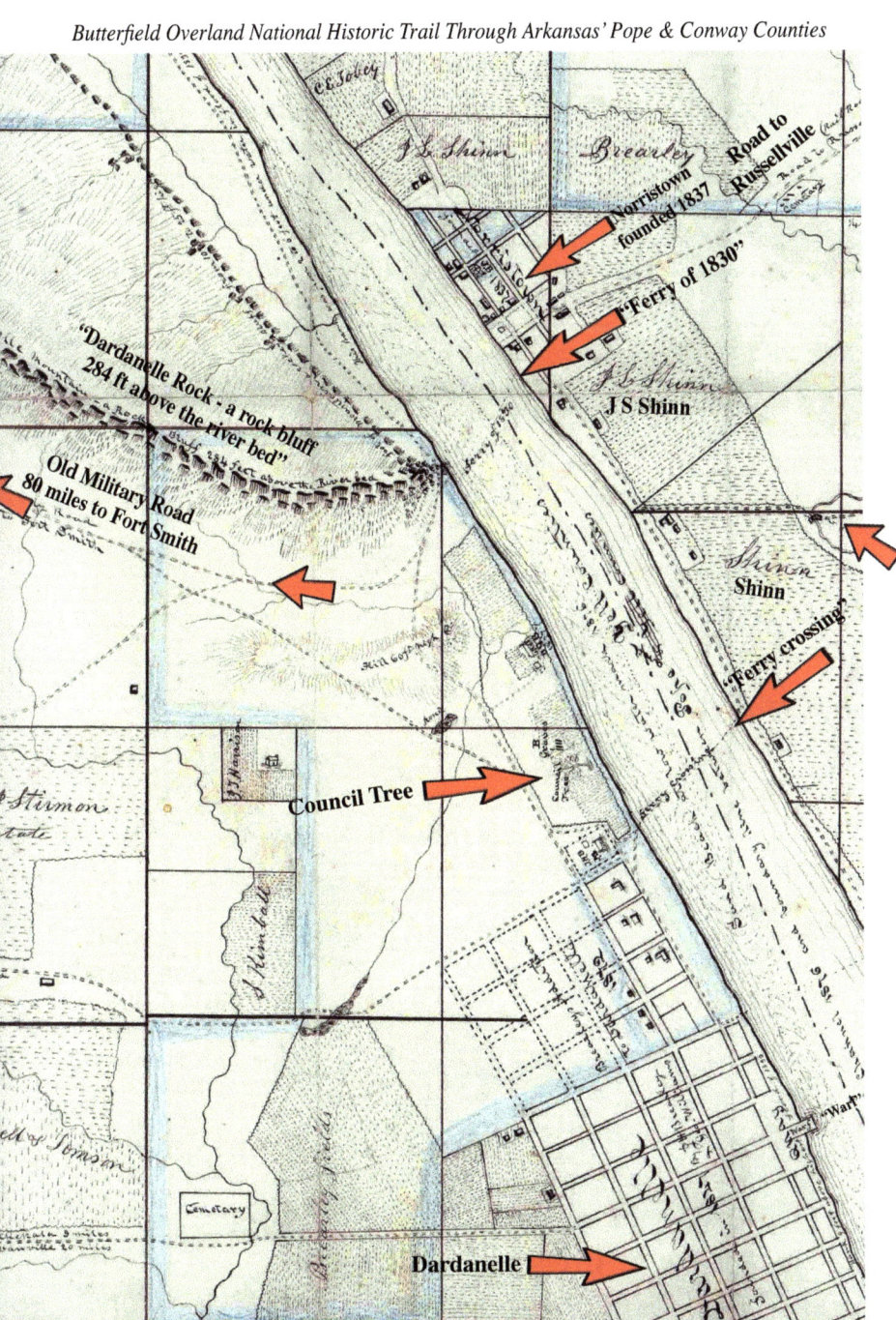

1877 map showing Dardanelle, Norristown and two ferry crossing sites.
Also shows Council Tree, 'Dardanelle Mountain,' and Military Road.
Map 0196, Map collection inventory, Arkansas State Archives, Little Rock, AR

In 1858, at Norristown, *"you could come almost to our door by stage from any direction. If you or your neighbors want to take a ride to California now a days you can come by us."*
In 1858, in a letter by Norristown resident C. C. Ewing, expressing pride in the Butterfield, writing to this sister, Miss Elizabeth Ewing of Pleasant Hill, Kentucky. *"They Sought a Land,"* by William Ragsdale, 1997.

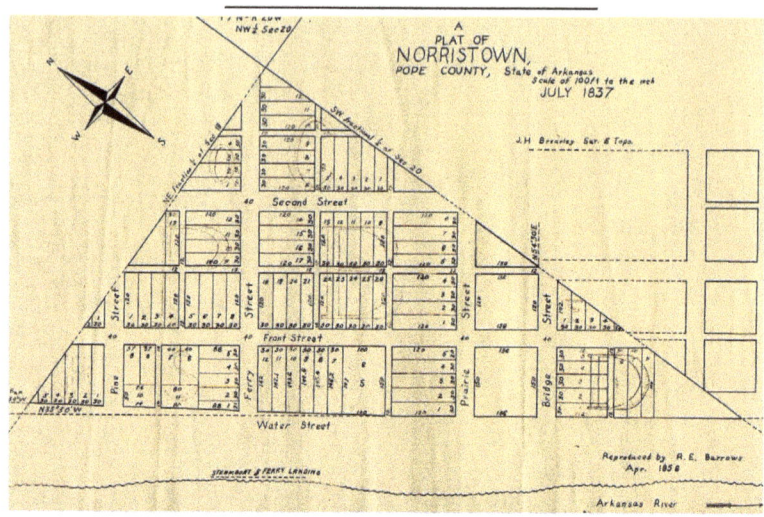

Plat of Norristown Streets, July 1837
Reproduced by R. E. Burrows, April 1856

This is the 1827 Dardanelle Ferry Site, north bank of Arkansas River
Photo by Bob Crossman, May 2024

Crossing on the Ferry

According to Wayne Banks, *"History of Yell County, Arkansas,"* as Butterfield's Overland Mail Co. stagecoach approached Norristown, the stage left the Mil-

itary Road and headed toward the bank of the Arkansas River about a mile south of the ferry crossing. Crossing on the Dardanelle ferry into Yell County, the stage followed the high ground south of Dardanelle Ridge passing through Mt. Zion and returning to the Military Road at Union Hill. To do this, a new road was cut through a settlement where the Nathans, Biggers, Huffs, Callans, Flurry, Ford and Chandley families had settled several years previously. From there the stage continued on westward to Stinnett's Station.
[*History of Yell County, Arkansas*, pg. 9]

At the time Butterfield's Overland crossed the Arkansas River by ferry at Dardanelle we do not know the ferry rates. However, just 12 miles downstream at the Galley Rock ferry, the rates as of January 25, 1858 as revealed in his petition to the court for a renewal license, are as follows:

For each wagon and two horses or oxen	$1.50
Four wheel carriage and one horse	75¢
Two wheel carriage and one horse	50¢
Each man with one horse	25¢
Each lead horse	10¢
Each loose horse or cattle	10¢
Each footman	10¢
Each sheep or dog	5¢

[*A Heart Within a Valley: A History of the Atkins Area*, by John C. Stroud, Centennial Bicentennial Committee, History Committee, 1976]

In 1869 the courts ordered for a ferry just upstream: *"...rates crossing the Arkansas River shall be double whenever the river is 12 feet above the ordinary stage of water. Is it further ordered by the court that said ferries respectively shall be furnished with good and substantial ferry boats at least nine feet wide and 36 feet long and furnished with side boards or railings at least four feet above the gunwale so as to protect stock from escaping from the boat. Boat to be provided with a good stiff at each ferry and one hand during low water and at least two good hands when river is high."*
[*Remembering Shoal Creek*, Ratha Burnham Lane, pg. 2, 1967]

As mentioned earlier in this book, on January 4, 1859, a correspondent for the San Francisco *Evening Bulletin* wrote about his experience at the Dardanelle ferry. He apparently deboarded the Butterfield owned stagecoach at Dardanelle, crossed the ferry on foot, and then boarded a Chidester owned stagecoach westbound toward Potts Inn and Memphis. He writes:

"When we reached Dardanelles (Dardanelle, Arkansas) it was late at night, and raining in an old-fashioned way... We were most unceremoniously turned out of the coach by the driver and delivered into the charge of the ferryman, who took the mail-bags on his shoulder, and, his lantern in hand, told us to follow up to this boat at the ferry landing, about one mile distant up the river... placing our blankets on our back, and valise in hand, the passengers proceeded to accompany him, through a torrent of rain... We all got soaking wet by the time we reached the coach on the opposite bank, and three of our party were considerably used up, next day, from the effects of the drenching." [San Francisco Evening Bulletin, Jan. 4, 1859]

"Pontoon Bridge across Arkansas River, Dardanelle, 2,345 feet long."
In operation between 1891 and 1929, it was referred to as
'The Longest Pontoon Bridge In the World.'
Original toll rates: 5¢ for a person walking; 15¢ for a person on horseback; 5¢ per horse or cow; 25¢ single buggy; and 35¢ for a double buggy.

A later Dardanelle Ferry, named "The Elva"
Pope County Library System, Katie Murdoch Genealogy and History Room of the Pope County Library System in Russellville, Arkansas,

Mike Goad reports that the steamboat Elva was used for operating and maintaining the pontoon bridge at Dardanelle, positioning the bridge segments, and chasing down sections that got loose in a flood.

The February 10, 1916 Russellville paper reports, "Having outlived her usefulness, the ferryboat "Elva" was beached on the Pope County side of the river at the crest of the recent record-breaking rise in the Arkansas, and now rests many feet above the level of the water. We've often heard, but never before appreciated, the expression 'as awkward as a steamboat on dry land.' Great Scott, what an ungainly sight old Uncle Noah's Ark must have made resting on the heights of Mt. Ararat! The old steamer will be dismantled, her engines removed, and the hull transformed into a freight barge."

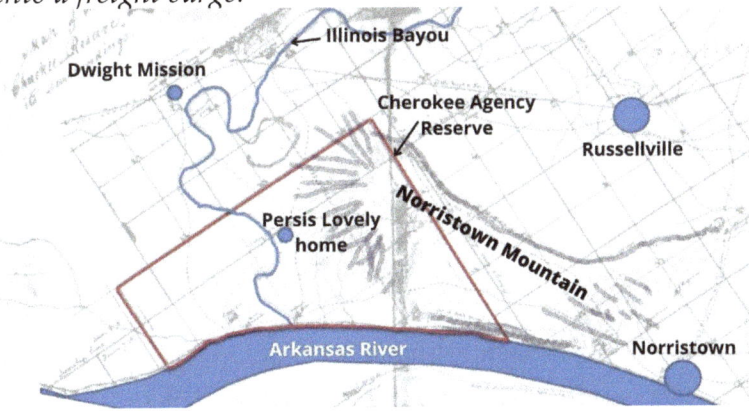

Image posted by Mike Goad

Latimore Tourist Home

In the 1939 edition of "The Green Book," Mrs. E. Latimore as the proprietor of a home that welcomed African Americans and offered them a safe place to sleep and a good meal - the only Tourist Home listed between Little Rock and Fort Smith, Eugene and Cora welcomed guests into their home from the 1930s to 1970s.

Norristown & Dardanelle Stations?

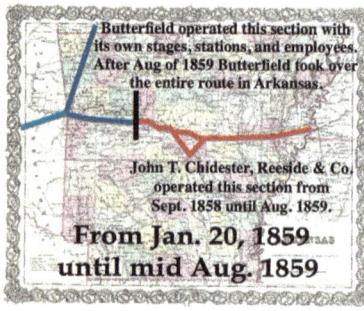

At the Dardanelle Ferry, there may have been a station both on the north and south sides of the river. Between Jan. and Aug. 1859, Norristown was the terminus for the Chidester stages and Dardanelle was the terminus for Butterfield stages. At terminus stops you would expect to find a station with fresh horses, employees, a spare stagecoach and parts for repairs. Also, in 1919 Charles T. Davis wrote about a former "change station" for overland stagecoaches at Dardanelle. Davis may have been referring to John L. Carpenter's Livery Stable, or John A. Croom Jr.'s stable in Dardanelle.

Norristown Today?

Today, the site of old Norristown is in the hands of the Corps of Engineers, and is called "Old Post Road Park." Retired Corps of Engineers employee Jack Johnson writes:

Jack Johnson

"In the U. S. bicentennial year, the wagon train which visited every state that year was to be in Russellville in 1976. The Pope County Historical Association of which I was a member put on a celebration at Arkansas Tech in the Dome. In addition, the Dardanelle Dam Site Park was to be renamed something bicentennial related. A contest was held among middle school students and a student won a $50 savings bond from the historical association with the entry "Old Post Road Park."

The US Army Corps of Engineers was to erect a commemorative plaque. So I was tasked to do the research and create exhibits. My supervisor said that it needed to be something functional as well, so I put a drinking fountain in the design. Still works!

Historic maps were the most conclusive illustrations and they were widely used. One such map indicated a cemetery on the road on what is currently international paper property on Highway 7T which is the Dardanelle Dam and Russellville project office access road. The map was accurate and included the gravesite of a Civil War soldier. It is probably lost to time, but I still know where it is. I was by the park a few years ago, and the exhibits have been upgraded."

Dardanelle
On the South Bank of the Arkansas River

Council Tree, South Bank of Arkansas River

The 'Treaty' of Council Oaks was signed on June 24, 1823, on what is now North Front Street in Dardanelle beneath two huge oak trees (102 feet high and 400–500 years old). Acting Governor of Arkansas Territory Robert Crittendon met with Black Fox, Wat Webber, Waterminnow, Young Glass and several other Cherokee leaders. Although Crittendon did not have official permission to negotiate any treaty, the Cherokee unwillingly surrendered their Arkansas land for a new tract of land in Indian Territory, signing the 'Treaty' June 24, 1823.

One of the two giant oak trees was destroyed in the early 1990s in a flood, but the other is still standing. The site is now a city park.

Photo by Darren J. Clay, 2023

Dardanelle Courthouse Fire April 21, 1913
The back of the postcard says, "Janelle with umbrella, Basil with paper near buggy."

Image courtesy of Arkansas State Archives

The Overland stage traveled on the Old Military Road from Dardanelle to Fort Smith. According to *"Little Rock to Cantonment Gibson Road"* in the Encyclopedia of Arkansas, the construction of that road was approved by Congress on March 3, 1825. The road was to travel north of the Arkansas River from Little Rock to Dardanelle (Yell County), avoiding Petit Jean Mountain and its surrounding bayous. It was to cross to the south of the Arkansas River at Dardanelle, to continue on toward Fort Smith and on to Fort Gibson. The total distance of the road from Fort Gibson in Indian Territory to Little Rock was surveyed to be 208 miles, 7 chains, and 72 links.

Early Dardanelle Street Scene
The community of Dardanelle developed on the south banks of the Arkansas River near the ferry crossing.

The Steamboat *Grand* at Dardanelle Wharf
The steamboat landing at Dardanelle, when water levels allowed, was a popular stop for steamboats between Little Rock and Fort Smith.
Source: Grissom Photo

STATIONS WEST OF DARDANELLE

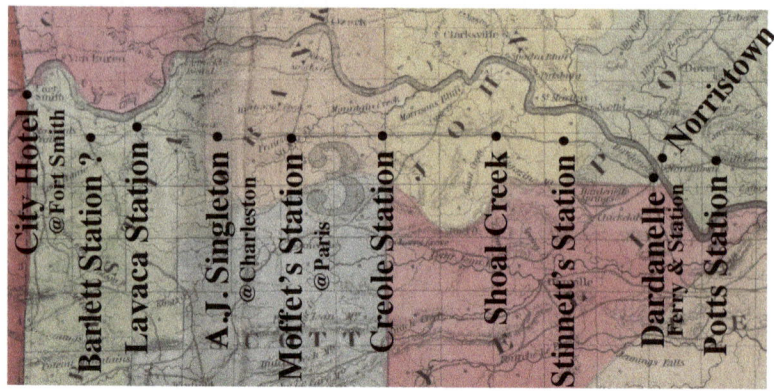

STINNETT'S HOME STATION

Leaving the Dardanelle Ferry and Station, heading west the stage would arrive at Stinnett's Station. There is an historical marker near the site of the Stinnett Butterfield Swing Station on Hwy 22, along the lake, west of Dardanelle in Yell County.

Approximate coordinates
N35° 16' 38.80" W93° 16' 28.37"

Stinnett Station Site Was on Opposite Bank of Stinnett Creek
Historical marker is in the center of photo.
Photo by Bob Crossman

Brief Description of the Entire 3,000 Route

The route across Arkansas often required detours due to poor road conditions and river levels.

The map on the following page, from the files of the Arkansas State Archives, shows some of the detours taken by Butterfield's Overland Mail Co. during 1858-1861.

Butterfield Overland National Historic Trail Through Arkansas' Pope & Conway Counties

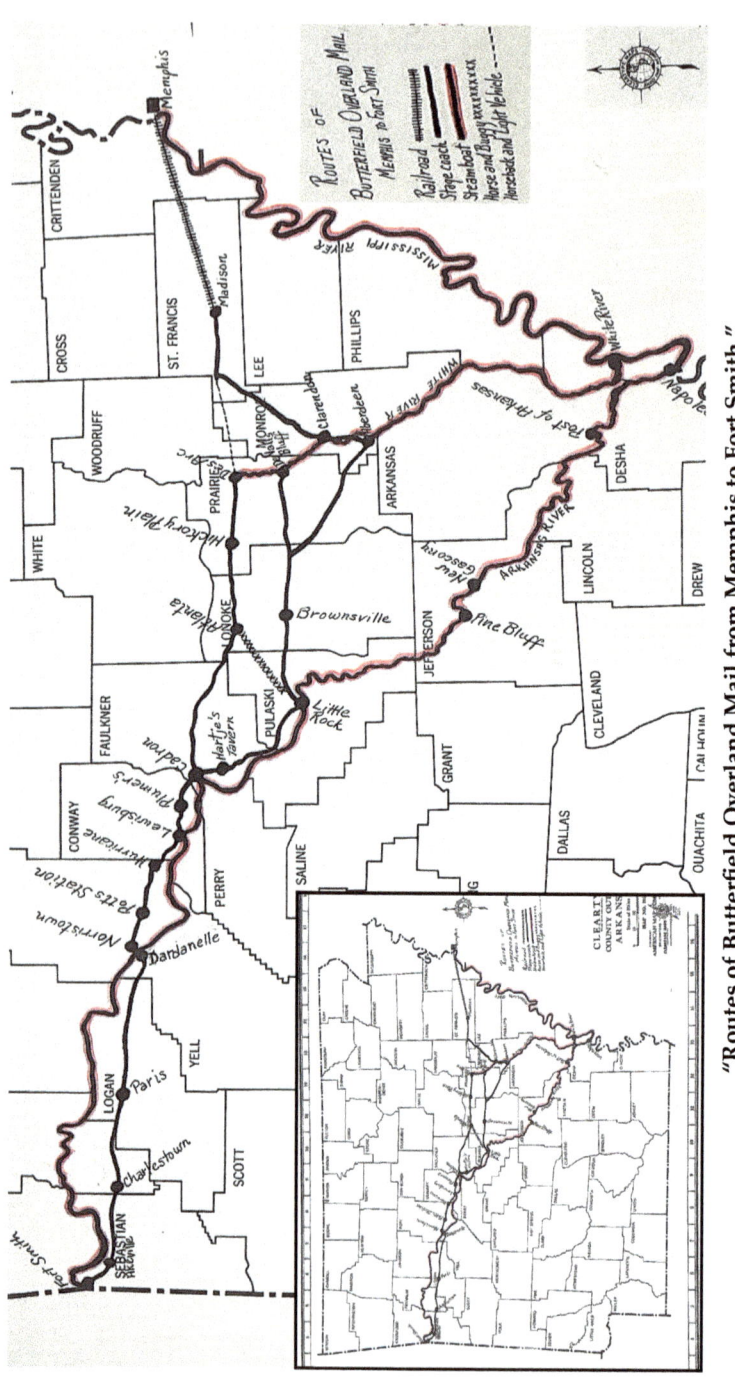

In Context With the Entire 3,143 Mile Route

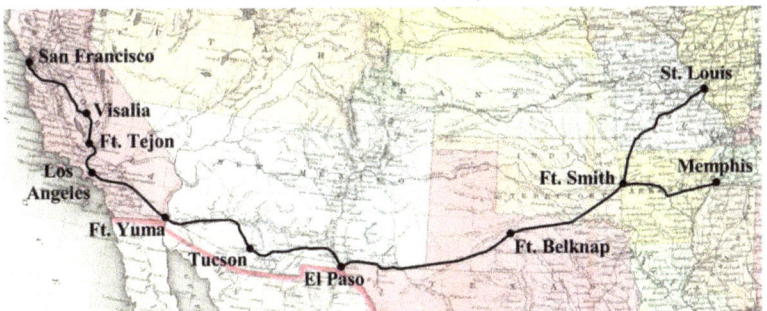

The Route from Memphis & St. Louis to San Francisco
Image Courtesy of "Mails of the Westward Expansion"

Arkansas was just one piece of the 3,143 mile route. The basic course of the entire route was set when Postmaster General Aaron Brown agreed with John Butterfield that the basic route would be from Memphis and St. Louis, merging at Fort Smith, and then to San Francisco.

Below is an 1857 map showing the two initial proposed routes from the Mississippi River to the West Coast.

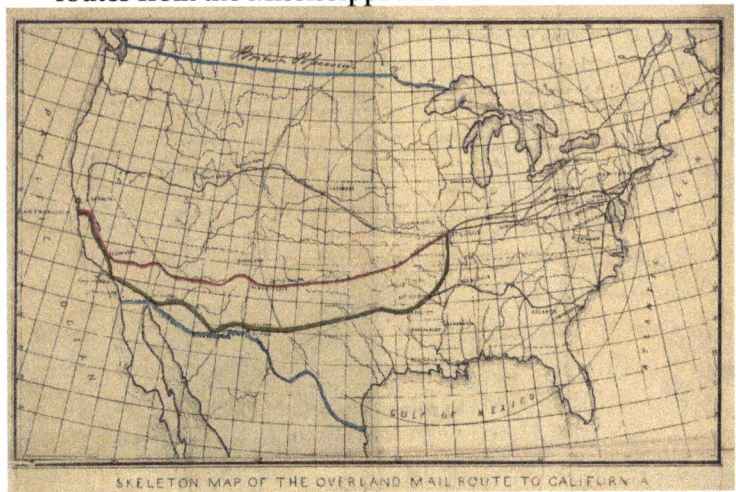

1857 Skeleton Map of the Overland Mail Route to California
The red route is the one proposed by John Butterfield when he bid on the contract. The green route is the one adopted by the Post Office Department. The thin lines out of Memphis and St. Louis indicate other routes or train lines in use at the time.

To work out the details of the exact route, two expeditions were sent out by the Overland Mail Company on January 2, 1858.

A eastbound expedition began out of San Francisco led by Marquis Kenyon. Others in that expedition included Frank DeRyther, S. L. Nellis, James Swart and John Butterfield, Jr.

A westbound expedition began about the same time out of St. Louis with George Wood, Jesse Talcott and Charles P. Cole.

The two expeditions were to meet at El Paso, Texas.

Completing their expeditions, they returned to Fort Smith on April 24, 1858, *"having made the trip from El Paso – a distance of 925 miles – in the unprecedented short time of twenty-five days, which we believe is the quickest trip ever made across the Plains."(May 1, 1858 Arkansas Gazette)* On this return trip to St. Louis, Marquis L. Kenyon made significant changes to the route recommended by the westbound expedition.

In June of 1858, with the preliminary survey complete: 1) a team began in California and another in Fort Smith, renting existing buildings or building new buildings to serve as stations; 2) horses, equipment and spare replacement stages and stagecoaches were distributed along the route; and 3) Daniel Butterfield fixed the schedule, setting arrival and departures to the minute from each of the major stations.

Butterfield established 139 stations in the beginning of service averaging about 15 miles apart, increasing to 175 stations within a year. The 34 mail stagecoaches, the Celerity wagons, and 150 other vehicles were spread along the route. John Butterfield employed almost 2,000 drivers, conductors, station-keepers, blacksmiths, mechanics, wheelwrights, helpers, hostlers, herders, veterinarians, armed guards, and harness makers along the route.

As of May 2024, the National Park System website (nps.gov) list the following stations on
The Butterfield National Historic Trail:

DIVISIONS OF THE ROUTE
East to West
9th Division —
  St. Louis to Tipton Missouri
8th Division —
  Tipton to Fort Smith, Ark., and Memphis to Fort Smith
7th Division —
  Fort Smith to Colbert's Ferry
6th Division —
  Colbert's Ferry to Fort Chadbourne, Texas
5th Division —
  Fort Chadbourne to El Paso
4th Division —
  El Paso to Tucson, Ariz.
3rd Division —
  Tucson to Fort Yuma, Calif.
2nd Division —
  Fort Yuma to Los Angeles
1st Division —
  Los Angeles to San Fransisco

MISSOURI STATIONS
St Louis Post Office
St Louis Train Depot
  by Pacific Railroad to the
Tipton Train Depot, *changing*
  June 1859 to Syracuse
  Feb. 1861 to Smithton
Schackleford's Station
Mulholland's Station
Burn's Station
Warsaw
Bailey's Station
Quincy
Yoast's Station
Bolivar
Smith's Station
Evan's Station
Springfield
Ashmore's Station
Smith's Station
Crouch's Station
Harbin's Station

ARKANSAS STATIONS
Northwestern Route
Callahan's Station (Rogers)
Fitzgerald's Station (Springdale)
Fayetteville
Park's Station
Brodie's Station (Lee Creek)
Woolsey's Station (Signal Hill)
Van Buren
Fort Smith

ARKANSAS STATIONS
Memphis Route
Memphis, Tenn.
Madison, Ark.
Des Arc
Atlanta (Austin)
Cadron
Plummer's Station (Plumerville)
Lewisburg (Morrilton)
Hurricane
Pottsville Inn
Norristown (Russellville)
Dardanelle
Stinnett's Station
Paris
Charleston
Fort Smith

OKLAHOMA STATIONS
Watson's Station (Skullyville)
Trahern's Station
Holloway's (Brazil Station)
Riddle's Station
Pusley's Station
Blackburn's Station
Waddell's Station
Geary's Station
Boggy Depot
Blue River Station
Fisher's Station
Colbert's Ferry

TEXAS STATIONS
Preston's Station
Sherman
Diamond's Station
Gainesville
Davidson's Station
Connolly's Station
Earheart's Station
Jacksboro
Murphy's Station
Fort Belknap
Franz's Station
Clear Fork Station
Smith's Station
Fort Phantom Hill Station
Mountain Pass Station
Valley Creek Station
Fort Chadbourne
Colorado River Station
Grape Creek Station
Camp Johnston
Head of Concho Station
Llano Estacado
Mustang Waterholes
Initial Northern Route
Horsehead Crossing Station

Immigrant Crossing Station
Pope's Crossing
Delaware Springs Station
Pinery
Guadalupe Pass Station
Crow Spring Station
Cornudas de los Alamos
Ojos de los Alamos
Hueco Tanks Station
Franklin (El Paso)
Later Southern Route
Horsehead Crossing Station
Fort Stockton (Comanche Spring)
Hackberry Hole Station
Barrilla Spring Station
Limpia
Fort Davis
Barrel Spring Station
Deadman's Hole
Van Horn's Wells
Eagle Spring
Fort Quitman
Birchville Station
San Elizario
Socorro
Ysleta
Franklin (El Paso)

NEW MEXICO STATIONS
Frontera (Cottonwoods Station)
Fort Fillmore
Mesilla
Picacho Station
Rough and Ready Station
Goodsight Peak Station
Fort Cummings
Cooke's Spring
Murphy's Station
Cow Spring Station
Soldier's Farewell
Station near Deming
Station near Lordsburg
Stein's Pass Station

ARIZONA STATIONS
Fort Bowie
Apache Pass Station

Dragoon Spring Station
Cienaga Station
Willcox's Station
Tucson
Pointer Mountain Station
Picacho Pass Station
Pima Village
Maricopa Wells
Gila Ranch
Murderer's Grave Station
Oatman Flat
Flapjack Ranch
Griswell's Station
Peterman's Station
Filibuster Camp
Swiveller's Ranch
Arizona City
Texas Hill Station

CALIFORNIA STATIONS
Fort Yuma
Pilot Knob Station
Mountain Springs Station
Cooke's Wells Station (Mexico)
Gardener's Wells Station (Mexico)
Alamo Mocho Station (Mexico)
Monument Station
Indian Wells Station
Sackett's Wells
Carrizo Creek Station
Palm Spring
Vallecito Station
Box Canyon
Blair Valley
San Felipe
Warner's Ranch
Oak Grove Station
Aguanga Station
Temecula Station
Laguna Grande
Murrieta
Temescal Station
Corona
Chino Ranch
San Jose Station (Pomona)
El Monte Station
Los Angeles

Butterfield Overland National Historic Trail Through Arkansas' Pope & Conway Counties

Cahuenga Station	Elk Horn Spring Station
Los Encinos	Hawthorne's Station
Mission San Fernando	Fresno City
Hart's Station	Firebaugh Ferry
King's Station	Temple's Station
Widow Smith's Station	Lone Willow Station
French John's Station	San Luis Ranch
Reed's Station	Pacheco Pass Station
Fort Tejon	Soap Lake (San Felipe)
Sinks of Tejon (Alamo Station)	Gilroy
Kern River Slough	Seventeen Mile House
Kern River (Gordon's Ferry)	Hernández House
Poso Creek Station (Posey Station)	San Jose
Mountain House Station	Mountain View
Fountain Spring Station	Redwood City
Tule River Station	San Mateo
Lindsay	Clark's Station
Packwood's Station	Oak Grove Station
Visalia Station	San Francisco
Cross Creek Station	Oak Grove Station
King's River Station	San Francisco

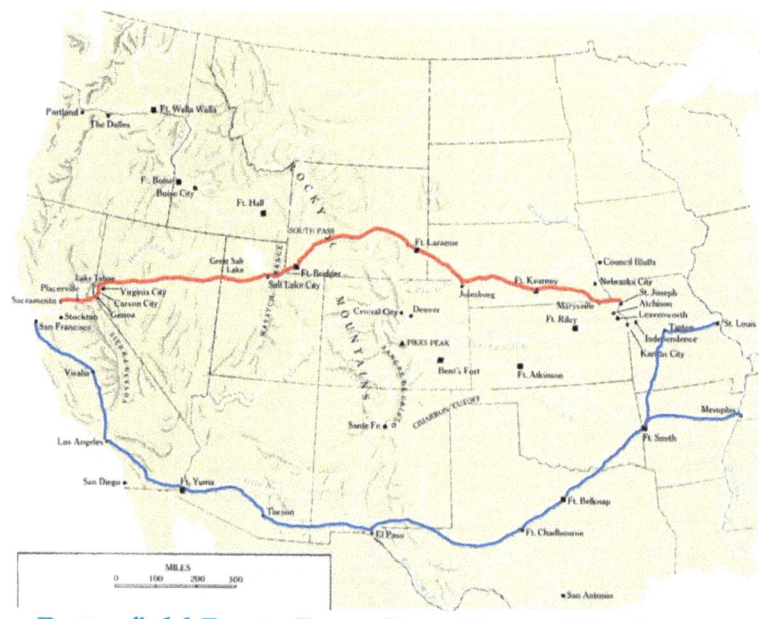

Butterfield Route From Sept 1858 to March 1861
Butterfield Route from July 1861 to Sept 1864
Map courtesy of Richard Frajola, "The Routes," page 3

ABOUT THE AUTHOR:

Dr. Robert O. "Bob" Crossman has lived in Faulkner County since 1988, when he and his wife established Crossman Printing near downtown Conway's Toad Suck Square.

He is a member of The Butterfield Overland National Historic Trail Association, Faulkner County Historical Society, Arkansas Historical Association, Southern Trails Chapter of the Oregon-California Trails Association, Shiloh Museum of Ozark History, Faulkner County Museum, Fort Smith Museum of History, Old Colony History Museum, and numerous philatelic societies.

After graduating from Russellville High School, Dr. Crossman received a B.A. from Hendrix College in Conway, Arkansas, and received graduate and post-graduate degrees from SMU in Dallas, Texas.

Bob Crossman is the author of seven books on the Butterfield:
- Butterfield's Overland Mail Co. STAGECOACH TRAIL Across Arkansas;
- Butterfield's Overland Mail Co. Use of STEAMBOATS Across Arkansas;
- Butterfield's Overland Mail Co. as REPORTED in the Newspapers of Arkansas;
- POSTAL HISTORY of John Butterfield's Overland Mail Co. on the Southern & Central Routes including Butterfield's Pony Express, 1858-1864;
- Butterfield Overland National Historic Trail PASSENGER DIARIES & STORIES Across Oklahoma, Arkansas, and Missouri, 1858-1861;
- Butterfield Overland National Historic Trail Through FAULKNER COUNTY, Arkansas, 1858-1861; and
- Butterfield Overland National Historic Trail Through Arkansas' POPE and CONWAY Counties, 1858-1861.

Dr. Crossman has four published articles on the Butterfield including:
- "The Butterfield Overland Mail Company: Faulkner County Connection," Faulkner County Facts & Fiddlings, Fall 2021, p. 24-32.
- "Fort Smith's Connection to the Butterfield's Overland Mail Co.: Stations Between Memphis and Fort Smith," Fort Smith Historical Society Journal, Fall 2021, p. 25-43.
- "I Lived on The Butterfield Mail Route for Decades and Didn't Know It," The American Philatelist, Jan. 2023, pp. 17-31.
  - Winner of the 2024 Mueller Award.
- "Faulkner County and Butterfield's Overland Mail Company Stagecoach Route," Faulkner County Facts & Fiddlings, Spring 2024.

The cemetery for the community at the old Green Grove steamboat landing is alongside THE BUTTERFIELD OVERLAND NATIONAL HISTORIC TRAIL in Faulkner County, Arkansas. Photo by D. J. Charles

© 2024 Robert O. Crossman

I just couldn't resist including photos of my family.

Bob & Marcia Crossman

Paul Crossman & Louis Lefebvre

Jessica, Blake Charles and Grayson with Bob & Marcia Crossman

Owen, David, Cooper & Marlie Crossman

Fred Borck, Raquel Borck, Brooks Bachamp, Bailey Bachamp, Dylan Bachamp & Sherry Borck

Gracie & Maggie Mae Crossman

My Golden Anniversary Edition of the 1929 Model A

Butterfield Overland National Historic Trail Through Arkansas' Pope & Conway Counties

Explore THE BUTTERFIELD OVERLAND NATIONAL HISTORIC TRAIL by also reading these books by Bob Crossman:

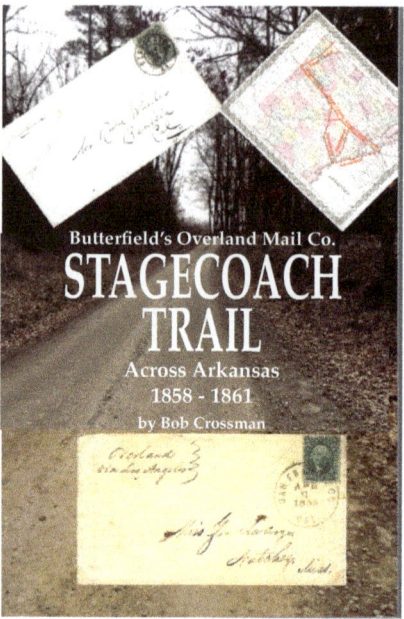

"Butterfield's Overland Mail Co. STAGECOACH Trail Across Arkansas"

This full color volume tells the story of the Overland Mail Company stagecoaches which carried passengers and mail west from Memphis and St. Louis to San Francisco through Arkansas. The Overland stagecoaches and stage wagons traveled day and night, completing the 3,293 mile journey is less than twenty five days.

This book pays special attention to each of the twenty Overland Mail Company stations spread across Arkansas. The stations were typically located about fifteen miles apart. The stagecoaches or stage wagons would stop for ten minutes at each station for the quick change of horses. Twice a day the stage would stop at a station for about forty minutes, allowing the passengers to have a moment of rest and purchase a quick meal while the driver obtained a fresh team of horses or mules.

"Butterfield's Overland Mail Co. use of STEAMBOATS to Deliver Mail and Passengers Across Arkansas 1858-1861"

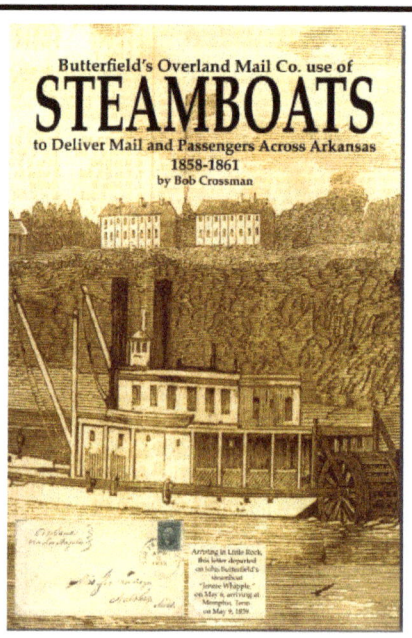

This volume explores the untold story of John Butterfield's use of STEAMBOATS to carry the Overland Mail over portions of the Fort Smith to Memphis route of THE BUTTERFIELD OVERLAND NATIONAL HISTORIC TRAIL.

While the purpose of my research of the Overland Mail was to satisfy my personal curiosity, hopefully this collection of my research will also make a contribution to the efforts of officially recognizing the route of Butterfield's Overland Mail Co. as a National Historic Trail.

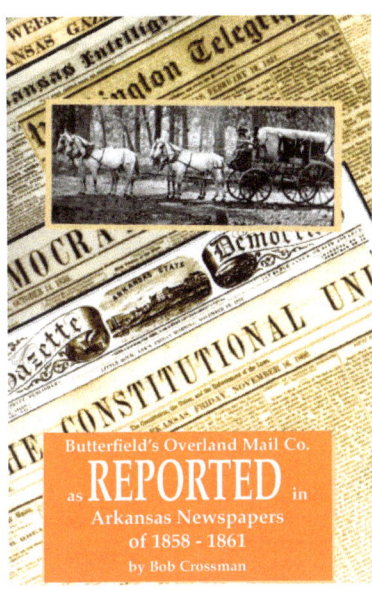

"Butterfield's Overland Mail Co. as REPORTED in Arkansas Newspapers of 1858-1861"

In this volume, the newspapers of Arkansas do an amazing job of covering the news around Butterfield's Overland Mail Company. Frequently the newspaper editors would draw their information from their exchange of newspapers across the country to bring to their subscribers the most accurate and comprehensive description of facts as possible.

In this book I have let the newspaper reporters tell the story in their own words. It has been difficult, but I have limited my interpretive comments to the brief title I've assigned each article. In this way, today's reader can immerse themselves into the world of the citizens of Arkansas back in the 1860's.

This new full color book reports on the mail carried by Butterfield's Overland Mail between September 1858 and March 1861 on the Southern Ox Bow Route, and beginning in July of 1861 on the Central Route. Also, to include additional information and artifacts from US transcontinental mail carried immediately before and immediately after the existence of Butterfield's Overland Mail Co.

In most instances within his previous three books on Butterfield's Overland Mail Co., Dr. Crossman focused primarily on the Arkansas route. This volume, by contrast, expands to focus on the entire route of the Butterfield. Also, by contrast, this volume focuses on Butterfield's presence on the Southern Ox-bow Route and later on the northern Central Route. In addition, this volume covers the entire time period of the Overland Mail Company's contract with the postal system: 1858 to 1864.

While the purpose of this research of the Overland Mail was to satisfy his personal curiosity, he is hopeful that summary of Butterfield Postal History will also make a contribution to Butterfield's Overland Mail Co. new status as a National Historic Trail.

"POSTAL HISTORY of John Butterfield's Overland Mail Co. on the Southern & Central Routes including Butterfield's Pony Express 1858-1864"

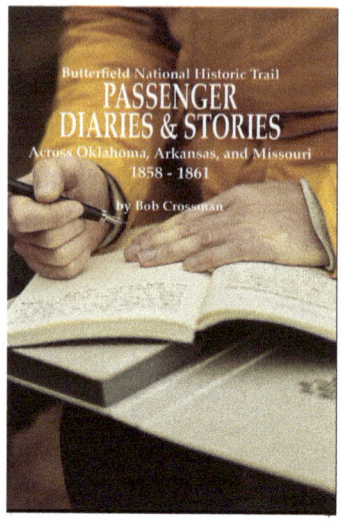

"PASSENGER DIARIES & STORIES across Oklahoma, Arkansas and Missouri"

Butterfield's Overland Mail Company stagecoaches rolled across Oklahoma, Arkansas and Missouri one hundred and sixty five years ago as they connected with San Francisco.

Now that Congress has named the route "THE BUTTERFIELD OVERLAND NATIONAL HISTORIC TRAIL," it seems appropriate for the Butterfield passengers to tell us about their experience on the trail. This book contains reminiscences and interviews of first person observers in their own words.

In most of the chapters of this book, the author only included portions of each original document that focus on passage through Missouri, Arkansas and the Indian Territory.

Some of the original source documents are hundreds of pages long and include details of passage through Texas, New Mexico, Arizona, and California that are not included here.

Several of the source articles were brief enough, *[such as Henry Everett, J. W. Farwell, Warren Baer, Thomas M. Johnston, and the speech by Waterman L. Ormsby]*, that the author included their full remarks concerning the entire route from San Francisco to the Mississippi River.

"Butterfield Overland National Historic Trail through FAULKNER COUNTY, Arkansas"

After twenty years of effort by the Heritage Trail Partners, and Arkansas Senator John Boozman, legislation was signed into law Jan. 2023 establishing THE BUTTERFIELD OVERLAND NATIONAL HISTORIC TRAIL.

That historic decision brings up the task of determining exactly where that trail crossed Faulkner County.

This full color book outlines the two year process Dr. Crossman followed to determine the exact route of THE BUTTERFIELD OVERLAND NATIONAL HISTORIC TRAIL across Faulkner County, Arkansas.

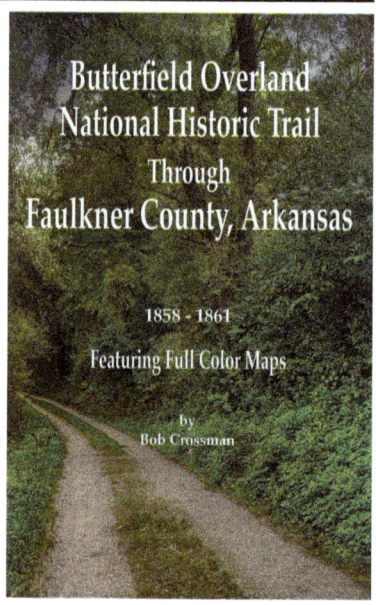

Also...
You Tube Videos by Bob Crossman
Open YouTube and search for the following titles:

"Authentic letters from the Butterfield Overland Mail"

"Butterfield Trail Arkansas Ferry"

"The Butterfield Trail across Arkansas"
Produced by the Oregon-California Trails Association

Milton Keynes UK
Ingram Content Group UK Ltd.
UKHW020906260724
446053UK00007B/21